COMPANION TO THE POOR

COMPANION
TO THE POOR

•

VIV GRIGG

An Albatross Book

© Viv Grigg 1984

Published in Australia by
Albatross Books
PO Box 320, Sutherland
NSW 2232, Australia
and in the United Kingdom by
Lion Publishing
Icknield Way, Tring
Herts HP23 4LE, England

First edition 1984

National Library of Australia
Cataloguing-in-Publication data

   Grigg, Viv.
   Companion to the poor.

      Simultaneously published: Tring, Herts:
   Lion Publishing
   ISBN 0 86760 019 5 (Albatross)
   ISBN 0 85648 891 7 (Lion)

      1. Missionaries — Philippines — Biography.
      2. Grigg, Viv. I. Title.

   266'.0092'4

Typeset by Rochester Photosetting Service, Sydney
Printed and bound in Great Britain by Cox & Wyman Ltd, Reading

Contents

Introduction

Before we begin...

People who write books usually write of successes. This is the story not of success, but of a search and a struggle: a search for the intimate knowledge of a hidden God whom, having found, we yet seek; a struggle to break out of a culturally-bound discipleship into a vision for discipling the millions of urban poor of Asia.

Prophets not only dream dreams. They have an inner compulsion to act out symbolically their prophecies. Their lives become cameos of truth, frescoes painted across the wall of grotesque evil. The cameos then become written parables.

This story is such a compulsive cameo, tooled into the darkest places of Asia: the unwanted, ignored, illegal slums of its great cities.

I could not write a theoretical, theological book aimed at the theoretically minded, for the God I know is not theoretical, nor a theologian of the standard teaching, book-writing kind. He is a *God of action*, whose thoughts and words cannot be divorced from his involvement in history.

It is this God of active justice, active power, active compassion who walked into the midst of poverty — in the person of a failing, fragile Son. And God wants to return, not once but a hundred times — in the lives of other faltering sons and daughters, who will confront the demons of poverty face-to-face in the name of the Lord of hosts.

This story has been written in the midst of all the phenomena that accompany a broken church. For a revival has swelled and captured the majority of the churches of New Zealand, the country of my birth, during these last fifteen years. Out of revival, missions are springing. The question in the minds of many Christian leaders is: 'Will this thrust be captured for effective ministry?' Hundreds of young people have been stirred. Sadly, many are taking short-term training, destroying years of their lives in the traumas of short-term assignments with inadequate supervision and structure.

This book is written with the desire to involve such men and women in long-term, productive mission to the unreached fields of Asia's slums. Already he has raised up a first wave of labourers, committed to lifestyles of voluntary simplicity and practical ministry in the midst of the poor. May these pages motivate a second wave to the other cities of Asia — people from other countries to establish new structures for mission to these poor. May it also challenge the leaders of existing missions to refocus on this new area of need, escaping the trap of decades-old strategies which have majored on rural ministry to the detriment of millions in the great urban metropolises who have gone without the word of God.

Asia's slum people are poor largely because of injustice and oppression. This book is the story of a rich Westerner trying to understand discipleship in the context of such injustice, poverty and corruption — incidentally, the social context of most of the scriptures.

Justice, discipleship and mission — if that sounds remarkably like Waldron Scott's central theme, don't be surprised. Scott was leading the Pacific Areas Navigators during my early training. He and Gene Tabor, who led the Philippine Navigator work for many years and is currently international director of the Lakas-Angkan Ministries, have worked closely together for years. Their ideas have been the framework of ministry in which I have been nurtured. Gene Tabor, Boni Arzadon and the Lakas-Angkan staff have provided the stimulus to develop many of these ideas — and initially gave me the opportunity and cultural training to pioneer this work. Jun and Milleth Paragas have been my special friends who have stood their ground to carry out the ministry at no little cost in reputation, health and status. God honours such men and women.

Others have influenced these ideas: Andrew Murray and 'Keswick' theology provided the basis of my early experiences of God; Warren Mason taught the mechanics of discipleship and ministry; Gene and Mary Denler graciously drew me into missionary life; Chuck Hufstetler gave hours of his life to mould me into a church-planter; John Waterhouse was willing to dare establish a publishing company at the edge of theological thought and rewrote much of the manuscript; my elders at Hillsborough Baptist, Bob and Prue Wakelin and Peter and Jenny Vos all gave me the time and quiet places to write. Thanks are due to Sarah Furniss who critiqued the manuscript and Shirley Clarke for her frequent retyping.

While the story is essentially unchanged, a number of names, dates and places have been changed for the sake of anonymity.

Go to the people,
Live among them.
Learn from them.
Start with what they know.
Build on what they have:
But of the best of leaders,
When their task is accomplished,
Their work is done,
The people all remark
'We have done it ourselves.'

Old Chinese Poem

1
City of Contrasts
THE CONFIRMING OF A CALL

I STEPPED OVER A MUD PUDDLE, ducked beneath a clothes line, then glimpsed the polluted river that surrounds the slums of Tatalon on three sides. I had searched, confused, for fifteen minutes amongst the labyrinth of concrete block and plywood houses before I saw the line of red, green and blue buckets leading to the hand pump. I stepped through a small gate to find people standing around, awaiting their turn and enjoying the early morning sun.

Two girls in patched dresses but black hair bright and neatly combed were sitting on their haunches, washing clothes in large aluminium basins. One looked up to see my fair skin and beard.

'*Si Jesus!*' (It's Jesus!), she exclaimed in Tagalog, the language of Manila, nudging her companion alongside her.

'*Hindi, kaibigan ko lang siya!*' (No, he's just my friend!), I laughed back.

I put my bucket hesitantly at the end of the line. As a stranger and a white person they motioned me, with Filipino hospitality, to the front of the line. One of the men worked the long handle up and down for me with great gusto. Being unsure of myself, I accepted the offer of help.

'*Saan po kayo galing?*' (Where have you come from, sir?), the girls asked with politeness, still laughing.

'I am living over in Aling Nena's upstairs room.'

'Why do you want to live *there*?'

I smiled. 'A few years ago I learned that Jesus said, "Blessed are you poor". I wanted to find out why the poor are blessed.'

There were nods and smiles of agreement, so I went on. 'I read too that Jesus came to preach the gospel to the poor. I want to preach the gospel to the poor, also.'

There were more nods and smiles. We talked and joked some more till my bucket was full. Sloshing water over my feet, I searched again for the paths back to my rented quarter of a squatter home.

Children looked at me shyly. I climbed the three steps up the eight-foot vertical ladder to my room. More water sloshed down the ladder. The bench that the landlady had left was a good place to sit and look out over my new-found community.

I reviewed the last evening.

The typhoon had come with the fury of the gods. The rain of sleet and the sound of crackling thunder seemed to be a final demonic onslaught to prevent me carrying my few belongings into the house. A bout of fever had attacked all day and no friend had been free or willing to brave the typhoon to assist in the move.

I had returned the jeep and retraced my steps to my new home by public transport in the dead of night. That first night as a squatter of Tatalon was spent dizzy, weary and sick. It was as if all the forces of oppression were being thrown against me in this endeavour to live amongst these men and women, the slum dwellers of Manila.

Three weeks before, in my diary, I had written this prayer: 'Lord, find me two rooms in Tatalon's slum area with cooking facilities and adequate sewerage. They need to be upstairs so that I might have a quiet place for prayer and study, and with windows to allow for a cooling breeze — before September the third.'

On September first I had been standing in this home talking to Aling Nena. (*Aling*, meaning 'older lady', is perhaps equivalent to the English 'Mrs' and is followed by a person's first name.) She was embarrassed at the poverty of the upstairs rooms she was offering, so she offered another as well — that used by her niece. The niece would move downstairs.

As usual, God had answered prayer: a room for myself, a room for companions and a small kitchen space — quite kingly for a squatter.

Having put back the boards to cover the entrance and finding a match and candle, I sat and gave thanks for the three windows that gave me a breeze and view out over the other homes. I was also grateful for the upstairs quietness and for the added touch of the Creator in the guava tree that grew outside the window in the midst of all this treeless expanse of plywood, cardboard, plastic bags and old tyres, used to weight down the rusty galvanized iron roofs. Somehow the tree symbolized the goodness of God in the midst of the evils of poverty. The lights in the window represented a source of hope in the midst of the dark oppression that is squatter poverty.

I was 'home' after twenty years. Years before I had seen clearly the direction my life was to take in the future. With the intensity of a vision, I had seen my destiny stretched out before me. It was a call direct from my Maker: to live amongst these people of the slums, to preach the gospel to the poor.

Out of the darkness

As I prayed into the dark hours of that first night in Tatalon, I wondered what the next steps would be. Silently I asked myself, 'How do you bring a whole city to the light? How can you rescue three million squatters and slum dwellers?'

As I prayed, a beautiful gold and white creature scurried along some smoke-blackened rafters of my new house. It was a well-fed rat, sleek and cunning. I watched him silently, intrigued and curious. My thoughts drifted to two pieces of wood used many centuries before. The cross of Christ was surely made of the same rough wood as this squatter home. Within the inner recesses of my spirit God seemed to be speaking — directly, personally:

'You'll save them by carrying my cross. It is an instrument of death. You must die to yourself in order to be a servant of this people.

'For unless a grain of wheat falls into the ground and dies, it cannot bear fruit. If it dies, it bears much fruit. This cross commands absolute authority over all people, all history, all cultures.

'Preach the cross! In it is the salvation of this people: from drunkenness and despair, from broken families and oppression, from poverty and desolation. In it alone is their hope.

'Remember, it is a rugged cross. Do not return to a tinsel cross. Take up my cross and follow in my footsteps, for I too chose poverty.'

The next evening my new seven-year-old girlfriend came shyly up the stairs. 'Would you join us? We are saying a *novena* for Aling Nena's husband.'

'What is a *novena*, Lisa?'

'We are praying so his spirit does not return to the house and annoy us! He died a year ago now.' Later, I would learn that, even after this *novena*, they would pray each year for his departed soul to leave and trouble them no more.

I was unsure of the correct response. 'May I bring my new Tagalog Bible and read from it?'

We climbed down the ladder and stooped into the doorway. About fifteen relatives were kneeling in front of the makeshift altar. An old lady chanted to the saints and icons that were laid out; they included a statue of the Virgin Mary. She was a professional chanter. The others joined in at appropriate times. There were a number of candles and other symbolic mementos placed neatly on the table.

I sat quietly and listened, trying to understand. At the finish they asked if I might have something to say. In halting Tagalog, I read the story of the resurrection in 1 Corinthians 15. It was my first sermon in my new language. They listened politely in obvious appreciation of my presence. No priest would attend a poor gambling family on such an occasion. I stayed for a snack of *pancit* (Chinese noodles), sandwiches and a cup of coffee, enjoying their laughter and friendship. This was the beginning of the spiritual transformation of this family.

The rugged cross had come to Tatalon!

Aling Nena was deeply honoured to have a foreigner and a 'man of God' stay in her house. Yet even she did not fully realize the import of those words of Jesus:

> He who receives you receives me... He who receives a prophet because he is a prophet shall receive a prophet's reward... And whoever gives to one of these little ones even a cup of cold water because he is a disciple, truly, I say to you, he shall not lose his reward (Matthew 10:40-42).

Aling Nena had been one of the original squatters. Twenty-five years before she had lived right on the banks of the river. As time went on, the original squatters rented out rooms in their homes to newer squatters. This provided a reasonable source of income. Those in the upper quarters of a house usually rented from the owners who lived downstairs.

Aling Nena was one of a clan, an extended family of about forty who lived in several houses around. She was also the chief gambler, operating a gambling den under my bedroom. I prayed for her to get converted! She was the first in the community to believe. Through Aling Nena, many gamblers heard of that cross. Many of her extended family believed.

Metro-Manila

Six years earlier I had stepped off the plane, the tropical humidity hitting me like a shock wave. It was my first time in Manila.

I was welcomed by friends, then driven the twenty miles across the city to my new home, along an eight-lane highway jammed and crammed all the way with cars, buses and trucks. It took two hours to travel through the towns and cities that ring Manila, beginning with Makati, the wealthy multinational and banking centre. Metro-Manila consists of four cities and thirteen towns.

The heat and smell hit me as we crossed the river, the pungent odour being overpowering. We passed by the rich mansions of Makati. Behind their brick walls, palm trees waved in the breeze. There were half-built concrete structures, towering office blocks and supermarts, movie theatres and little old shacks; rivers and fuming buses that crazily raced against each other, pouring out enough dirty black smoke to cover a man in half a minute. The houses decreased in size as we drove through the poorer city of Caloocan and moved down a side road into the town of Valenzuela. Finally, we were out into one of the middle-class subdivisions. We drove into a beautiful Spanish-American style mansion behind a concrete and iron paling fence.

Four hundred years before, the Spanish had conquered this archipelago of 7000 islands scattered in the South China Sea. They named it after their reigning monarch, King Philip. The Malay peoples dwelling there were scattered around the islands, speaking over a hundred different dialects. Arab traders had converted many of the settlements (called *barangays* or *barrios*) to Islam. But behind the Spanish sword marched the Spanish cross of Catholicism. Many priests lived heroic and saintly lives for the gospel. Others were the spearhead of the exploitation of the people.

In 1898 the Filipinos threw off the Spanish yoke, only to be taken over by the Americans in 1901. Along with their education, their medical systems and their new patterns of free-trading exploitation, the Americans opened the door for a new wave of missionaries.

The first Filipino believers were stoned. At times Bibles were burned. Nevertheless, thousands responded to the gospel, experiencing a new freedom in Christ from the old bondage of animism and Catholicism. However today, 84% of the population remain Catholic-animist. The culture, even the modes of speech, are deeply influenced by the need to appease or utilize the spirits,

Some megopolises in Asia (excluding Japan and China)

City	Population (thousands)	Country
Calcutta	8,827 (1980)[1]	India
Bombay	8,343 (1980)[1]	India
Ho Chi Min City	8,114 (1979)[1]	Vietnam
Djakarta	6,397 (1980)[1]	Indonesia
Hong Kong	4,900 (1979)[2]	Hongkong
Manila	6,200 (1980)[3]	Philippines
Karachi	5,005 (1980)[1]	Pakistan
Bangkok	4,999 (1979)[1]	Thailand
Delhi	3,170 (1971)[4]	India
Madras	3,170 (1971)[4]	India
Singapore	2,362 (1979)[4]	Singapore
Bangalore	1,653 (1971)[4]	India
Hyderabad	1,769 (1971)[4]	India
Colombo	2,700 (1970)[2]	Sri Lanka
Pusan	2,450 (1975)[4]	Korea
Surabaya	1,336 (1971)[4]	Indonesia
Bandung	1,201 (1971)[4]	Indonesia
Taipei	2,150 (1970)[5]	Taiwan
Dacca	2,064 (1974)[4]	India
Rangoon	3,662 (1973)[2]	Burma
Kuala Lumpur	451 (1970)[4]	Malaysia
Lahore	2,165 (1972)[4]	India
Ahmenadab	1,741 (1971)[2]	India
Poona	1,135 (1971)[2]	India
Jogyakarta	2,490 (1971)[2]	Indonesia

References:
1 *Year Book, 1981, Encyclopedia Britannica*
2 *Stateman's Year Book, 1980-81*
3 *Philippines Year Book, 1979*
4 *Demographic Year Book*, United Nations, 1979
5 *World Urbanization 1950-70*, Kingsley Davis, University of California, 1969

the saints, the Virgin Mary, God himself and all those in authority or close proximity.

Like other urban centres in Asia, Manila has undergone rapid change. The *barangay* that was an Arab and Chinese trading post became the Spanish Fort Santiago in Manila and later the centre of American-Japanese warfare. Today the original centre is surrounded by the bustle and laughter of over eight million Metro-Manilans, some enjoying their fortunes in magnificent mansions, others seeking theirs, while yet others seek to eke out a living to overcome the perpetual hunger that drives them on.

One of the cities, Quezon City, is the centre of bureaucracy and government for fifty million Filipinos, while Manila City itself is a bustle of Chinese businesses, import-export businesses, street-hawkers and one million students, crammed twelve per room. The density of central Manila today is over 58,000 people per square kilometre. Thousands of gaily-decorated jeepneys (converted World War Two jeeps seating seven along each side at the back) move through the main streets, filling the city with fumes and loud music.

Supporting the growth of this steaming megopolis is a highly productive and mineral-rich land, roughly the size of New Zealand. Rice, corn, cassava, sugar, bananas and pineapple grow readily. The country exports coconut oil, clothing, electrical equipment, metal ores, fruit and vegetables, timber and sugar. But the forests have been rapidly destroyed, leading to flooding of formerly rich agricultural provinces during the twenty typhoons that savage the country yearly. The minerals are also rapidly being exploited by the richer nations.

Muslim rebels in the south and a growing New People's Army of Marxist guerillas in a number of provinces pose a constant threat to the armed forces of the brilliant, autocratic President Marcos. Until the assassination of Senator Benigno Aquino in August, 1983, he had brought relative stability and progress to his country where an American-style democracy had only led to chaos.

The country, ruled by 400 rich families, has a gross national product of only US$450 per person (compare Australia US$7,340, New Zealand US$4,370, USA US$8,620[1]), but the poor are very poor and the rich are very rich. The urban poor increased from 24% to 40% between 1971 and 1975. The total poor in the country grew from 38% to 45%.[2]

Yet life expectancy is 60.5 years (due to the American emphasis on expensive medical facilities and some years of stable government). Of the total population forty-three per cent are below fifteen years of age. The population is expected to double to 90 million within twenty-three years.[1]

Manila is also a highly educated society with over one million students in college and university. The country has an overall literacy rate of 87%. Practical and technical training are developing rapidly to provide a base of expertise for industrialization.

During the decade of martial law in the seventies, major infrastructure projects in Metro-Manila were completed. There are now concreted highways, effective sewerage and water, and telephones that often work. There is a sense of progress, of development. The population of this city has exploded since the war — at a rate of five per cent per year from 1.7 million in 1950 to 6.2 million in 1980 and an estimated 10.8 million by the year 2000.[3]

But there are areas of horror within the city, particularly 'the tourist belt' with its opulent hotels, its brothels, its discos and all the lust and slavery that goes with the deflowering of a nation's beauty — ironically a country once known for its modesty. The putrid, turpid rivers are filled with gaseous effluents emanating from thousands of uncontrollable factories. Against a modern city skyline is the less appealing backdrop of hundreds of hastily constructed shacks made up of packing cases and plywood, taking up every vacant lot or public place.

Yet even man cannot destroy all of God's beauty. The gold and pink hues of Manila Bay sunsets continue unabated. Outlying suburbs on rolling hills twenty miles from the centre of the city enjoy cooling breezes, the landscape dotted with trees and grass.

Above all the Filipino soul, with its capacity for adaptation unequalled by any nation on earth, survives all the traumas of urbanization, relocation, exploitation and unemployment with a *joie de vivre* and a romantic, poetic optimism. Should God, friends, fate, Virgin, saints and spirits be favourable, the poor may also move into a bureaucratic job and middle-class subdivision.

Urbanization
Among the spectres of poverty, few can match the endless spreading slums of the sprawling Third World megopolises.

Since the industrial revolution, almost every major city has had its share of squatters and slum dwellers. Earlier this century the

European nations to a large extent were able to cope with this problem through increased exploitation of Third World resources, the creation of the welfare state, emigration and industrialization.

But the post-war phenomenon in Asian, African and Latin American megapolises is an apparently unresolvable conflict between over-urbanization, due to *too rapid* a migration of millions to the capital cities, and industrialization which is *too slow*, providing too few jobs. The migrants have only swelled the ranks of the under- and unemployed. The way in which the new urbanites have adjusted themselves to their environment is by creating permanent slums, the extent of which is now far beyond the control of any planning or administrative body.

The number of Asian cities with a population of more than five million will rise from ten in 1980 to twenty-nine by the year 2000 and their combined population will increase from 80,000,000 to 300,000,000.[4] In most of these megapolises the slum population will make up an increasing percentage of the total rising from present rates of 30% up to 75% in some cities.

For example, when the slum population of Manila began growing during the sixties it made up a quarter of the population. In the eighties it will make up over 40%. Squatter numbers have risen from 23,000 in 1946 to over two million today, increasing at a rate of 12% per year.[5] Peter Lloyd writes:

> The greatest rates of growth for squatters have occurred in national capitals. Industry, dominated by transnational companies, has preferred the capital city — often a seaport and close to the political leadership of the country, technical skills and services are more readily available, and the city elite providing a greater part of its local market. The government bureaucracies administering the expanding social services are largely located in the capitals. So instead of a hierarchy of urban centres evenly spaced along a continuum, we find the capital cities embracing an ever-increasing proportion of the national population, far outdistancing their nearest rivals.[6]

Metro-Manila, for example, is eight times the size of the second largest Filipino city, Davao.

Slums of hope
The physical characteristics and culture of each shanty town (slum, squatter community, *favelo* or *bustee*) differ from country

to country. Yet the process which generates them and the resultant evils are universal amongst the major cities of Third World countries.

There are two kinds of slums thus generated: [6]

(a) The inner city slums
These are the decaying tenements and houses in what were once good middle- and upper-class residences. These he describes as generally being 'slums of despair' to which gravitate those who have lost the will to try and those who cannot cope. Yet here, too, are recent immigrants who have come to be near employment opportunities and students in their hundreds of thousands, seeking the upward mobility of education.

In such an atmosphere of despair and downwards deterioration, the social forces and expectations work against a responsiveness to the gospel. So it appears more strategic to turn to the second kind of slum when social forces and expectations create a high degree of receptivity to the gospel.

(b) The peripheral shanty towns
These spontaneous communities built around massive cities tend to be 'slums of hope', whose longer established occupants have employment and are now seeking to build their own homes. Yet here, too, there are people and clusters of despair.

The shanty town of Tatalon in Manila is an example of one of the many slums that have sprung up since World War Two. It lies halfway between Manila City and Quezon City, two cities that are part of Metro-Manila.

Barely noticed in the thick of the ownership controversies that have taken place over the past forty years has been the steady growth of an unwanted population in Tatalon. A total absence of facilities and services notwithstanding, a good number of provincial migrants flooding into the Metro-Manila areas found the unoccupied lands of Tatalon ideal sites for establishing footholds in the big city.

The average home in Tatalon contains 12.3 people. There are 14,500 in this community which takes up just six blocks — a density of 57,500 people per square kilometre. The homes were first put up by the river. Because of regular flooding, many were relocated on higher ground.

Tatalon is, however, one of the more fortunate squatter areas. The government in the last few years has established a sites and services programme, gradually upgrading the area. It has put in roads, a number of toilets and some water pumps, surveyed the land and organized the people so that those longest in residence could buy the small lot on which they lived. This is at a cost of between 70 and 120 pesos per month over a twenty-five year period (US$1 equals fourteen pesos). This program has evolved from a responsiveness to people's needs over a number of years.

Tatalon is a place of hope, a slum in which to dream and to aspire, a community that is beginning (with a lot of help) to come through decades of suffering into a little economic security. Enough progress is being made in obtaining land and water, enough individuals in the community have found employment to spur the others on. In such a context, the gospel is welcomed as one more social change people are going through. It can move like wild fire.

Rugged labourers

When we consider such numbers of people living in such destitution and squalor, hoping against hope for a future of economic security, we are reminded of the Master:

> When he saw the crowds, he had compassion for them, because they were harrassed and helpless, like sheep without a shepherd (Matthew 9:36).

Must we not also pray that he who 'came to preach the gospel to the poor' will send out the workers to reap this over-ripe harvest?

God's method is people! Do we not hear a call to go as servants of that rugged cross, labourers whose delight is work, sacrifice and suffering, whose souls are filled with compassion and whose lifestyle is that of simple poverty?

In the next few years there needs to be an evergrowing stream, a new thrust to these dirt-and-plywood jungles. We need bands of people who, on fire with the message of Christ's kingdom, will choose a *lifestyle of simplicity* to proclaim that kingdom to the *poorest of the poor*. These bands can include people at different life stages or of different marital status, but primarily men and women who deliberately choose singleness for a period, or couples without children or whose children have grown up. Together they will form 'cells' or 'communities' of six to ten workers to go to each of these great Asian cities.

Training of these teams needs to occur in the sending country. Upon arrival in the host city, there needs to be a full year of language study and continued orientation. During this time these teams will be split up, going two-by-two to different squatter areas. They will then gather together one day a week for relaxation, mutual ministry, further training and celebration of the Lord's Supper at a retreat centre, led by an older mature couple with pastoral and administrative oversight for the 'community'.

We need men and women willing to commit themselves to this task initially for six years — this being long enough to establish a first church — but with the *intention* of spending fifteen to twenty years in the urban community to establish a discipling movement.

It is not unreasonable for a young person to believe God that his life might bear fruit during these fifteen to twenty years. Is it a big enough request to ask God for 1500 new Christians — or 3,000 or 15,000? Such would be a worthy lifetime's work. There are many who have seen God do this elsewhere.

In 1898 Hudson Taylor, with the vast needs of inland China in mind, issued a call for 'twenty able, earnest and healthy young men willing to consecrate five years of the lives to itinerant work, without thought of marriage or of settling down till their special work is accomplished'. We need a similar breed of Christians for today's 'new' mission field of the Asian megopolises.

If that is a realistic goal for young people, can we not expect more from older couples? Grey hairs carry much weight in Asian societies. Older, middle-aged couples whose children have left home can have great impact. For such adjustments — physical, emotional, cultural — are much harder, but this can be offset by maturity, acceptance in the community and skills learned over the years.

Younger couples may need to delay having children until they have had time to establish themselves in these slum communities and know how to cope with the poverty, the drunkenness, the food, the climate and the hatred and how to raise children in such an environment.

The task ahead
Christ's commission commands us to 'disciple the nations'. This is our mandate: to bring these slum communities under the authority of the kingdom of God.

Our methodology is that of preaching the good news of Jesus, teaching the whole counsel of God and establishing disciples in worshipping, economically stable fellowships.

Let us trust God to provide converts, disciples and leaders. We need to see churches properly nurtured, squatter discipleship and vocational training strategically placed and effectively led, and the gospel free to transform the economic, social and political life of these slum areas.

Economic transformation is an immediate pastoral concern. Compassion demands that we not only pray for but also *give* to the poor. Evangelism cannot be done outside of compassion. Economic programs on their own, however, do not appear to extend the kingdom when used as a basis for evangelism. On the other hand, the discipling process involves dealing with a person's environment, as well as with his personality. It is insufficient to save people's souls when their environment forces them back into spiritual slavery.

One critical issue is the lack of industrial skills within the squatter areas. We need skilled tradesmen, carpenters, fitters and turners, electronics specialists and people with management skills to set up smallscale workshops to train men. We need to motivate the churches and aid organizations to provide the equipment for such work. As well as choosing lifestyles of personal simplicity, we need to be managers of the wealth of our rich friends at home, tapping it wisely for the uplift of their new poor brethren.

It is insufficient to develop economic projects while ignoring issues of oppression, exploitation and injustice. We are commanded to do justice (Micah 6:8), to defend the rights of the poor and needy (Proverbs 31:8,9), and to be intercessors (Isaiah 59:15-16). Housing is one such issue which requires proclaiming the gospel to government officials and teaching them the biblical basis of community development, city planning and honesty on construction sites.

In maintaining a commitment to righteousness and social justice in the context of legalized oppression and exploitation, we may at times have to be aligned with particular political groups. But such a commitment will be primarily pastoral. Ultimately we have no political ideology except that of the justice and righteousness of the kingdom of God — a stance which, in practice, is not apolitical. This sort of responsible, politically aware pastoral care may be unpopular with the evangelical church, with its phobia of Marxism and secular humanism. It also will be dangerous for those of us working in the slums, particularly under right-wing or

Marxist regimes. Wisdom and caution are always needed, but withdrawal from the complexities of life is not an option open to 'suffering servants'.

Those choosing simplicity to reach the poor need to continue to put priority on proclaiming the kingdom and teaching the scriptures rather than getting locked into the social and economic programs they generate.

Short-term specialists may be of help in such projects but in general, wandering youth are not an asset.

Such ministries will also take on a high degree of the miraculous for where there is the cross there is power.

Behind all these is the need for men and women in the home base, committed to a simple lifestyle, to evangelism, and to the poor and needy, who will maintain base communities for the sending and receiving back of such men and women.

In each team the gifts needed are infinite: a comics designer, an apostle-evangelist, or an apostle-pastor team leader, an administrator, or a poet-communicator, a specialist in establishing small-scale industries... But above all men and women with a drive and a zeal and the training in the practice of establishing the Kingdom of God — who can preach and disciple, consolidate small bible studies and establish multitudes of believers into movements of disciples. Men and women with eternity in their hearts, the promises of God in their souls, and the fire of holiness in their spirits. Men and women of a rugged cross.

The apostle Peter was such a man. He walked in a poor man's wooden sandals (Acts 12:8) and had no gold for the beggar at the Temple (Acts 3:6).

Similarly the apostle Paul underwent stonings, beatings and shipwrecks, living 'as poor, yet making many rich' in his desire to reach the cities of his world.

The story tells of Toribio of Mexico who, barefoot, traversed Mexico. The Mexicans called him the poor one because he was evidently poorer than they. He learned the Aztec language quickly and preached fluently in that language. The Indians loved him like a father and regarded him almost like a divine Inca because of his total commitment and absolute poverty. He covered 40,000 miles on foot. He had nothing of his own to leave behind when he died.

Above all we need to remember the Master, who calls us to walk in his sandalled footsteps, he who chose poverty in birth, poverty in life and finally, blood dripping from thorn-crowned brow, chose poverty on the cross of a criminal.

Who will go? Who will take up their cross and follow him? Who will give fifteen or twenty years of their lives for the poorest of the people in the slums of Asia? Who will live amongst them, love them and show them their King? Is this such an unreasonable request from the Lord who gave his all?

Footnotes on Chapter 1

1. The Data Sheet, Population Reference Bureau, Washington, DC, 1980
2. 'The Poverty Puzzle', *Far Eastern Economic Review*, March 27, 1981
3. *Philippine Yearbook*, National Economic and Development Authority Manila, 1979, p 115. The 1950 figure is quoted from David Kingsley *World Urbanization 1950-1970*, University of California, 1969, p 234
4. 'Food and Population', Asia 1981 Yearbook, *Far Eastern Economic Review*, p 43
5. Morris Juppenlatz, *Cities in Transformation*, University of Queensland Press, St Lucia, Queensland, 1970, pp 97-102. Figures are taken from 'Squatters Growth in Metro-Manila Based on the 1963 Count of Squatters' UN-PHHC Housing Research Team. These are the latest official figures as of December 1982.
6. Peter Lloyd, *Slums of Hope? Shanty Towns of the Third World*, Pelican Books, 1979, pp 21 and 33. Reprinted by permission of Penguin Books Ltd.

2
Never the Same Again
FACE TO FACE WITH POVERTY

I WAS IN A HURRY. Like the priest in the story of the Good Samaritan, I was rushing to get some time alone with God. As I strode through the jostling, crowded streets, from the corner of my eye I glimpsed a lady begging. I brushed her off, catching just a memory of her grey hair.

She grabbed my arm, looking at me with an old lady's offended dignity in her eyes. I pulled away again and rushed on, but I could never forget that face. It was hardworking, framed in white hair. And something more. It was a blue-grey face, the face of a sick and dying woman.

I hurried on, haunted and confused.

But God didn't rush on. He faced the face of poverty. He entered in. He became a man and dwelt amongst us. His cross stands in the midst of suffering. It is a cross of compassionate involvement. If we would take up that cross, we too must enter in to the need, we too must dwell in the midst of suffering and poverty.

In this cross is meaning, reality and destiny. Only in this cross are there ultimate answers to the deep questions that are the wellspring of life and human existence.

Rugged cross or jewelled replica?

I first learned of the impact of that cross on the poor of Asia's cities as a questing ten-year-old in the uppermost garret of Dunedin's oak-panelled public library. There I found a treasure trove of biographies of famous Christians.

One was to set the direction of my life. It was the story of a sickly (most great missionaries seem to have this quality), bespectacled man. It was the story of Toyohiko Kagawa of Japan.[1]

Kagawa saved cities. He had compassion.

As a student he quickly came to see that if the slum people of neighbouring Shinkawa were to be saved, he must live *amongst* them and preach the gospel. The poor would never accept something that was offered by the wealthy and respectable who came from across the river, dispensed their charitable gospel and then went back home. The church must be planted in the slums and tended day and night.

On Christmas Day 1909, Toyohiko Kagawa, aged twenty-one and frustrated after efforts to persuade his superiors of the needs of the poor, packed his belongings into a little handcart, crossed the bridge of 'the Singing Cicada' and walked into the slums of Shinkawa to serve his Lord. For the next fourteen years and eight months he lived there: teaching, preaching the gospel and ministering to the poor.

As a result, Kagawa later became a strategic figure in the development of the labour unions of Japan, brought widespread reforms to stem the flow of poor to the cities, was a key man in the reconstruction of Tokyo after it was devastated by the 1923 earthquake, helped fashion a law that abolished slums and was a leader in the reconstruction of Japan after the Second World War.

In all these activities he was constantly proclaiming the cross. He established nationwide evangelistic campaigns, preached to the country's political leaders and to the Emperor himself, and established many churches and Bible schools amongst the poor. Thousands entered the kingdom through his life.

It was a child-learned truth, an unquestioned assumption learned from Kagawa that living amongst the poor was the only possible strategy for one who would plant the Christian faith amongst them.

Kagawa chose the rugged, rough-hewn cross of his pauper Master. He chose the suffering of the cross. Being wise, he could have been rich. His chosen poverty shows his true wisdom.

We, too, must reach these millions of poor. The cross is our method, the cross is our message, the cross is our life.
Kagawa once wrote:

In the blood-drops dripping
Along the sorrowful road to the Via Dolorosa
Will be written the story of man's regeneration.
Tracing the blood-stained and staggering footprints
Let me go forward!
*This day also must **my** blood flow, following*
In that blood-stained pattern.[2]

Unfulfilling discipleship

During my first year in Manila I had lived with a missionary and his family, serving and learning from him, and assisting in his ministry of teaching discipleship in a Bible school. I taught two classes of sixty students. In order to disciple some of these, I recruited nine students to join me in a venture establishing a predominantly middle-class church, all of us working under an experienced missionary.[3]

Theologians and church growth specialists would say that this was the forefront of missions, the cutting-edge of the great commission, the thick of the battle to establish new beachheads for the gospel.

But my life was unfulfilled. The philosopher within found no answers to the search for meaning; the artist found no fulfilment in the search for perfection and ultimate truth; the leader had not found the centre of destiny and purpose towards which to lead others. All three components told me I still was far from the place of God's call.

I was relatively proficient at passing on skills and programs, reproducing labourers who could pass on skills and programs to young believers. But I was not transferring the discipleship of Jesus. The students came from poor families. For many, Bible college became the stepping stone to economic security as a paid 'professional' pastor. My own wealth, and our deliberate focus on a middle-class target group, precluded me from passing on the disciplines of the Beatitudes: poverty of spirit, meekness, peacemaking (bringing justice with love) — those qualities that are the heart of discipleship.

It was only a half-size cross I was transmitting: I realized my life must portray a dramatically different picture of ministry if I was to lead these men and women into the way of the cross. Discipleship had to be taught in the context of a Jesus-style ministry to the poor — in the context of rejecting pride and status-seeking, power and economic security.

A thief in the slums

This search for meaning, destiny and truth came into sharp focus the week I spent travelling to the home of one of my students. He lived in the slums of a pineapple factory in Mindanao, the large southern island of the Philippines.

We travelled by jeepney. Four people sat in the front seat, seven sat along the sides and another four hung precariously along the back in various ways — all laughing and talking in unknown dialects. There was a load of vegetables on my feet, the chickens squawking under the seat. As we passed a military outpost a soldier cautiously inspected each passenger, then climbed abord the front seat to give protection. Villagers looked at us sadly from small nips huts huddled along the road.

Finally, we arrived at Lario's home on a pineapple plantation, stretching for mile after mile on land confiscated or bought by oppression from hundreds of peasant farmers. The accumulated profits are taken out of the country to America, by juggling them between three different companies. Meanwhile the 7000 workers, many of them former owners of the land on which they now worked, lived on a pitiful wage in a square mile of squatter homes. At least, argued the transnational company, they *had* some income. But the factory deliberately kept this below subsistence level in order to circumvent union troubles. We Westerners eat the canned pineapple produced, with little thought for the social and economic ramifications.

Lario's house consisted of bamboo posts and pieces of wood he had scrounged from the dump and elsewhere. As I stooped through the door, the first thing I did was put my foot through the floorboards.

They called in all their *utang* (the debts of old friends) to feed me and gave me their blanket, a mosquito net and a sleeping mat.

Lario's mother and father both worked. His father was ill, with skin diseases on his legs. Their income could not provide enough money for medicine.

The toilet had blown over in a typhoon, so we began to dig a deep hole. The neighbours came to see this *Americano*. They had never seen a white person work with his hands before.

'Hey, Joe, what are you doing?'

'I'm digging a toilet. Why don't you come over this evening. We will preach the gospel and explain why!'

In the afternoon, I talked with Lario's mother. As she ironed with a charcoal iron, she told the story of their poverty, of the personal tragedy that had caused it and the oppression that had perpetuated it. Tears fell. She told of how the Lord had sustained her, how in him alone was her comfort.

As evening came, smoke from the wood fire wafted through the house, driving away the mosquitos. Estella, Lario's twelve-year-old sister, picked up the home-made wooden guitar and began to sing of the Lord who understands the pain and sorrow of his children, who is building a mansion 'just over the hilltop'.

'*Mahirap*', she said to me sadly, 'life is a so hard, so poor.'

In the light of the kerosene lamp, we ate our rice and fish for supper. Then we placed a lantern outside and set up some bamboo for seats. It was Easter Friday, so I began to speak of the cross.

The lantern cast its eerie light on to the tattered clothes of the men sitting on the bamboo seats we had made. It was quiet. One could sense listening ears of the neighbours in the surrounding houses as they sat in their windows to listen. They knew of those nails through his wrists, the jolting of that wooden post as they dropped it into the ground, the blood flowing from that crown of thorns.

As I spoke of the thief beside Jesus as he cried 'Jesus, remember me', and of Jesus' reply, 'This day you will be with me in paradise.' I was aware of the power of God within and about me. A big denim-clad youth sitting at the front, named Samson, began to quietly weep. In his repentance, the Spirit of God entered his life. For he, too, had been a thief.

In the midst of this twentieth-century scene — surrounded by the poor, in the presence of the Spirit of God, declaring the cross — I was aware that I was standing in the central stream of history. For two thousand years earlier before a similar village congregation, a poor scribe had stood in a similar pair of dusty sandals, declaring his destiny in the words: 'The Spirit of the Lord is upon me because he has anointed me to preach the gospel to the poor' (Luke 4:18).

And here the pauper apostles of history had stood through the centuries. Here was meaning, destiny and truth, enough to satisfy the deepest searchings of the human heart.

For the proclamation of that cross stands at the centre of all meaning. In it justice and truth, mercy and compassion meet.

That cross is framed by suffering, by poverty and by the pain of humanity. It is framed by the poor.

That night my own heart found rest. From that night there could be no turning back from God's call to enter into his purposes in history. I *must* preach the gospel to the slums.

In a heap of ruins

But we need something deeper than the search for ultimate meaning and reality to drive us on. That driving passion is to know and to love him who loves us.

The dignity, the human quality of the leadership of Jesus had captivated me as a child and brought me into his kingdom. God had overwhelmed me with his love.

But once having known him, we continue to seek him, 'counting everything as loss because of the surpassing worth of knowing Christ Jesus our Lord'.

Where then can Jesus be found today? To find him, we must go to where he is. Did he not say, 'Where I am, there shall my servant be also'?

Such a search invariably leads us into the heart of poverty. For Jesus always goes to the point of deepest need. Where there is suffering, he will be there binding wounds. His compassion eternally drives him to human need. Where there is injustice, he is there. His justice demands it. He does not dwell on the edge of the issues. He is involved, always doing battle with the fiercest of the forces of evil and powers of darkness.

The question I asked was: 'Where would Jesus be involved if he were in Manila?'

One day I stood on the top of a one-hundred-foot-high mountainous pile of rotting, decaying food and rubbish. I looked at the shacks of 10,000 of Manila's poorest and at their emaciated figures scavenging paper, bottles and cans to resell them to middlemen who would then recycle them.

The people had work — they were happy in that. I watched as little children, older women and comparatively healthy workers picked their way through the pile. Then they carried their goods in sacks on their shoulders back to their homes. Here the goods were sorted and classified. The smell was indescribable. Sickness was rife. The houses were constructed from old sacks, metal and other old garbage.

The children reached out their hands in laughter to touch me, but I began to weep. In anger, I cried out, 'Lord, how long can you permit the degradation and destruction of your people? Why don't you do something?'

The Lord was not slow to respond. As quick as a flash I knew his answer: 'I *have* done something. Two thousand years ago I stepped into poverty in the person of my Son. And I have dwelt there ever since in the person of my sons and daughters. Today I am calling for other sons and daughters to enter into the poverty of the poor in order to bring my kingdom to them.'

Jesus would dwell today wherever there is need. Here the Prince would become one of the paupers:

> For you know the grace of our Lord Jesus Christ, that though
> he was rich, yet for your sakes he became poor that by his
> poverty we might become rich (2 Corinthians 8:9).

Here he would preach, heal and bring justice.
Job described these poor:

> Yet does not one in a heap of ruins stretch out his hand,
> And in disaster, cry for help?
> Did I not weep for him whose day was hard?
> Was not my soul grieved for the poor? (Job 30:24-25).

It was in slums such as this smouldering rubbish heap of
Tumbakan, a modern-day urban Gehenna, that Jesus himself
would minister.

Four hundred communities

General Tobias, general manager of the National Housing
Authority, has described how by 1978 the NHA had identified
415 squatter communities such as Tatalon in Metro-Manila: some
better, a few worse. Of these 253 can be upgraded on site. The
implication was that the demotion and relocation of unwanted
squatters by truck-loads of armed men would proceed in the
remaining 162 communities.

Yet Jesus would have ministered to these very people. Surely we
too must live amongst them, bringing them the tangible blessings
of the kingdom. His compassion compels. The cross compels. The
search for meaning and reality compels.

We must call men to that task and place the cross where the
battle is being hardest fought. The church must not only be
planted; it must be planted where the gospel has never been
known. And where is the hardest place to plant the church, but
amongst the poor of these cities? We must establish poor people's
movements, squatter churches, squatter evangelists and pastors,
and scores of celebrating fellowships.

Yet our ideals are constantly limited by the realities of our
humanity and its incipient sinfulness, both personal and
collective. Identification with or amongst the poor cannot be
accomplished in a day, a week, or even a month. A missionary
must always limit his own idealism. I needed to move in a new
direction harmoniously with the body of co-workers in which I
found myself. Because my mission's structures pointed in other

directions, because I needed to learn new skills and because I was limited emotionally, physically and socially, the attainment of that calling would take time.

Footnotes on Chapter 2

1. Comments on Kagawa are taken from Cyril J. Davey, *Kagawa of Japan*, Epworth Press, 1960
2. Toyohiko Kagawa, 'The Cross of the Whole Christ', in *Meditations on the Cross*, SCM, 1936, p 16
3. For a study of this church-planting venture see Cary Perdue, 'The Case of the Kamuning Bible Christian Fellowship,' *Asia Pulse*, Evangelical Missions Information Service, Box 794, Wheaton, Illinois 60187, July 1982, Vol. 15, No. 3.

3
God's Happy Poor
THE POOR IN THE SCRIPTURES

I WAS SITTING IN A MOSQUITO-INFESTED ROOM in the depths of despair. Suddenly, ten years of our life's work had disappeared. Ten years of building relationships, moulding ideas, ministering to each other and building towards what we believed was a near perfect multinational missions structure had collapsed about our ears.

The issues were complex and I knew I did not fully comprehend. But as I understood it, the problem related to this need 'to preach the gospel to the poor'.

To understand what Jesus wanted us to do for the poor, I sat down with a friend one day and copied out every verse in the Bible about the poor on to small, white cards. I carried them with me for four years. They were my meditation day and night: they determined every major decision.

Questions continually rolled around my mind: 'Why are the poor, poor?' 'Why are they blessed?' 'Which poor are blessed?' 'Why does James call them rich in faith?' 'Who are the poor Jesus spoke of?'

My concordance to the Bible listed 245 references to 'the poor', 'poverty', or 'lack' in the English scriptures. They made an interesting study. I observed there were six main root words:[1]

Ebyon	— needy and dependent (61 times)
Dal	— the frail poor, the weak (57 times)
Rush	— the impoverished through dispossession (31 times)
Chaser	— to suffer lack of bread and water, to hunger (36 times)
Ani	— poverty caused by affliction and oppression (80 times).

The word Jesus uses in the New Testament for 'poor', *ptochos*, is the translation of the word *anaw*, which in turn is derived from *ani*.[2] *Anaw* at times means 'the humble', but elsewhere, as in Isaiah 61:1 from which Jesus quotes, it has the meaning of 'the oppressed poor'.

The concept of poverty and the analysis of its causes and effects change as the history of God's dealing with his people progresses. Before the monarchy of David and Solomon, in the Pentateuch and in Job, societies were built essentially around extended family or clan structures. Riches were the blessing of God; poverty was brought about by some misfortune or through judgment of personal sin. The poor man was to be helped from his poverty.

From the time of the monarchy, a centre of privileged people began to develop. Excavations in Tirzeh indicate that before the monarchy all houses had similar dimensions and furnishings. During the 8th century BC however, different districts had come into being: a well-to-do neighbourhood for the rich; slums for the poor.

The rich began to treat the poor as though they belonged to a lower order. Poverty came to be seen as a much deeper deficiency in a person, particularly in the Wisdom literature (the Book of Proverbs and so on).

The poor, for their part, began to see their poverty as synonymous with being oppressed. The standard expression, 'who oppress the poor', attributes the cause of poverty to the rich.

Hence we find the prophets denouncing constantly the rich (called the oppressor or the unrighteous) and upholding the 'godly poor'.

These are the *ani*, the oppressed poor with whom Jesus identified — 'the poor of Yahweh'. 'Poor in spirit' is an expression primarily describing this social class and its response to such oppression.

Leaves off the bushes

Some time after the mission had collapsed, I had returned to the Philippines to work with some of my former co-labourers who, because of their commitments to the poor of the Philippines, had established an indigenous discipling movement known as the *Lakas-Angkan* (the strong clan). In returning I determined to refuse to be trapped by mission expectations into a middle-class missionary lifestyle. I must dwell amongst the poor. I must enter into the knowledge of God. I must learn to die to self, to security, to my own culture, to my wealth.

The first step was to learn the language and culture of the poor.

I arrived in a small city out in a Tagalog province in a crowded bus. Here I was to study the language of Manila's poor, Tagalog, in one of its purest provincial forms.

I prayed: 'Lord, I have no home here, no contacts, but I'm sure you'll provide. Find me the poorest families. Since I'm unused to living amongst the poor, let it be a well-built home, with a good toilet so I can maintain my health.'

There was one church in this town of 100,000 (apart from the historic Catholic cathedral, sadly full of images). I walked down to the pastor's house and asked for accommodation for a few days. He was gracious, but could ill afford to provide for me. My respect for him knew no bounds, for I had known this man as a fine preacher in a city church. He had chosen to minister to the rural poor at no little cost.

After a couple of days, the pastor's assistant came to take me to his home. We travelled by tricycle (a motorbike with a highly decorated and stylized sidecar costing about 5c a ride) along the half-formed muddy tracks into the unfinished government subdivision. The local wisdom was that corrupt government officials had embezzled the development funds through various means. All down the track I met shy smiles and calls of 'Hey Joe!'

At the house, I thanked the Lord. It was perfect.

Ka Emilio, the old man (he was sixty-eight years of age) told how the family had constructed the house in one week at a cost of $130. It was all I'd prayed for: concrete walls and a tin roof (Filipinos call it a G.I. sheet). The toilet had a concrete floor, with enough room to shower on by scooping water with a tin can from a plastic bucket. The old frog and some neighbourly lizards kept it clean. Next to my bedroom was the community pump.

We put in a bunk above my friend's bed and pushed out the wall six inches since I was ill-suited to a Filipino-sized bed. This gave us a good five-by-six foot bedroom to share.

Ka Emilio was a man of old Tagalog dignity, a gracious and hospitable host. He coughed constantly, for one lung was rotten with tuberculosis. He maintained his health by his industry in planting and watering vegetables and the trees around his home.

I knew no Tagalog, he knew no English, but we had many long conversations. Once he described for me the Japanese invasion of their city, complete with dive bombing and its effects on the frightened people, all in dramatized Tagalog. He taught me much of the dignity and pride of the Tagalog people whom I had come to serve.

I ate next door at his daughter and son-in-law's home, but often I would watch Ka Emilio cooking his rice. At times all he had to eat with his rice were the leaves off the trees he'd planted.

Job 30:3 tells us of such poor:

> Through **want** and hard hunger they gnaw the dry and desolate ground; they pick mallow and the leaves of bushes and to warm themselves the roots of broom...

Ka Emilio was one of the *chaser*: those who lack the basic necessities of life, those who lack, those who want.

At nights I would lie sweating on my plywood bed and search for answers. 'Why was he poor?' 'How could such a poor man be blessed?' A study of the word *chaser* told me some causes of this kind of poverty.

Proverbs tells us that wickedness causes the belly to suffer want (13:25); too much sleep and want will attack us like an armed robber (5:10,11); hasty planning leads to want (21:5); oppressing the poor to increase our own wealth, giving to the rich, (22:16); loving pleasure (21:17) or miserliness and gambling (28:22) all bring us to want. This poverty is caused by personal sins.

The scriptures also speak of the solution:

> The Lord is my shepherd, I shall not want (Psalm 23:1)
> Those who seek the Lord lack no good thing (Psalm 34:10)

His son understood such promises. One day through an evangelistic crusade, Ka Emilio came to believe that Christ had died for him.

I gave him a Tagalog Bible in comic form (the poor read comics, not books). Perhaps time would lead him to a complete obedience to this Lord who is Shepherd, and this would lead him and his family out of want.

But I knew even then, that such a solution was insufficient. There are deeper causes to such poverty than personal ones: communal and national and global problems requiring biblical solutions at each appropriate level.

But I needed, along with Jesus, to begin at the level of the personal and spiritual and explore outwards. First we explored rabbit-raising. I bought a goat for Ka Emilio to supplement his income, but he eventually sold it, as he was too old to constantly take it out to feed. Ultimately, the solution for Ka Emilio was a son who got a job in Saudi Arabia and sent back American dollars!

Dog stew

Some poverty is caused by sin. But poverty also *causes* sin. The broken social structure of the squatter areas creates an environment which exercises little social control over sin.

One result of poverty is that it causes people to steal.

Proverbs 30:8-9 offers this sound advice:

> Give me neither poverty nor riches; feed me with the food that is needful for me, lest I be full and deny thee, and say 'Who is the Lord?' or lest I be poor and steal, and profane the name of my God.

A favourite meal in the Philippines, to go with the beer, is cooked dog meat. One day I was walking round the corner of the track and came across three men quietly pushing a jeepney loaded with dogs. They had stolen them and would sell them to a restaurant for meat.

That same week I walked past a big Roads Board truck. They were draining it of gasoline. Poverty causes us to steal.

Ninety per cent proof

Poverty also causes drunkenness. The first thing one notices amongst areas of poverty is drunken men. Everywhere there are groups of men drinking — at all times from morning to night. Drunkenness and alcoholism cause destitution, but most drunkenness amongst the squatters is a result of the poverty in which the men find themselves.

Unemployment results in drunkenness. Even Proverbs indicates this. When it advises against kings becoming drunk, it suggests:

> Give strong drink to him who is perishing, and wine to those in bitter distress; let them drink and forget their poverty, and remember their misery no more (Proverbs 31:7).

(We ought to be careful not to interpret this as a licence for the poor to drink, but rather as a plea for sober kings!)

An environment of unemployment is a surface prescription for drunkenness. One Filipino study of a slum community indicated that 68% of the employable adults are unemployed.[3] In Tatalon it was 42%.[4] Drinking with friends is a way to fill up the day and drown out the sorrow, despair and lack of self-respect inherent in unemployment.

Ka Emilio's two sons became my good companions. Living with them began to reveal some of the inner workings of poverty to me. Seraphim had been a soldier but lost his job and income for two years because of a wound. In my diary one night I jotted:

Tonight Seraphim will drink himself to sleep. It is hard to be without work. If he had work, he could get married. His girlfriend is already working and has graduated. He melancholily plays his guitar on the doorstep as the sun sets. A man of dignity, a soldier of honour seeking to maintain his dignity with the Beatles and a bottle. How do I help his soul and body? How can this poor man be blessed except in the kingdom?

What is the solution to drunkenness? Some years before I had travelled through a valley in Bukidnon. The homes were amongst the poorest I had seen — thatch huts, but only a few metres square. I asked around to discover why.

There was a local rice wine which was ninety per cent proof. Everybody drank it. The women were pregnant at thirteen or fourteen years. The children were born to drunken mothers and so grew up with the taste and desire for wine. People died before they were thirty. So it went on for generation after generation.

Then an older lady missionary had come in and started an orphanage. From this base people had fanned out, preaching the gospel. The preaching of the gospel had broken that cycle. These *chaser*, those whose personal sins have caused poverty, are blessed by receiving God's kingdom.

The poverty of immorality
Poverty provides an environment not only for drunkenness, but also for immorality. In the immediate cluster of houses around our home, very few couples were legally married. Many of the women had lived with two or three husbands. A number of men had a *kabit* (a second wife). In one survey we did informally, over thirty per cent of the men indicated that their becoming squatters had

been caused by some form of immorality — often in the process of 'eloping' or taking a new wife and hence leaving their provincial home.

The squatter area seems to be the ultimate collecting pot for the moral outcasts of society. Perhaps this is because they are areas where social norms and values have broken down almost totally, immorality and infidelity running unchecked and unashamed.

In a survey of the forty-three neediest families in one slum area, only one sixth of those interviewed had been legally married when first living with their wife.[5] Six men and four women had been previously married.

Types of initial union	Total number of families	% of sample
Church marriage	2	4.65
Civil marriage	5	11.63
Living together	4	9.30
Elopement and living together	17	39.54
Cheated and living together	7	16.28
Raped and living together	7	16.28
Polygamous household	1	2.32
Total:	43	100.00

The figures are each a symbol of pain, anguish and frustration.

This was typically expressed the day I was sitting in my upstairs room, preparing a message in Tagalog. Suddenly, an angry upset voice was heard in the rooms below: 'I'm going to leave him! I'll file a law suit!'

Two or three neighbouring relatives rapidly materialized to quieten down their neice, each passing on a piece of advice.

'The best thing is to stay with him,' one lady said. 'I remember when I first heard that the *Bombay* [Manilan terminology for an Indian — her late husband had been one] had another woman. I was furious. So I followed his jeepney and watched. They met at a bookstand, so I went and talked nicely to her. I didn't let her know I was his wife. She told me she had three children also. I have even had her children in my home when she could not cope!'

Her daughter added her own story: 'I cried for months when the father of my son married her, but I've learned to forgive.'

But the woman in distress would not be quieted. What could she do? He had another woman! There were many discussions during the next few days as the women sat for hours at a time, analysing what options were open when their common-law husbands moved on to the next woman. Would they remain faithful themselves? Or find another, kill him, or shift elsewhere?

Immorality creates poverty by generating bitterness, jealousy, insecurity, family disorganization, hatred and murder. It is difficult for a man to adequately support more than one family. When relationships have been destroyed and broken, it is difficult for the children to learn how to relate to any form of authority, or develop the management skills necessary for many jobs.

Personal sins help create poverty. Poverty, in turn, provides an environment for personal sin. This kind of poverty is only transformed by a gospel and a discipleship that enables people to be freed from these sins.

Deaf and dumb stowaway

Of course not all poverty is related to personal sins. The words ebyon and *dal* describe another kind of poor. *Ebyon* is the designation of the person who finds himself begging: the needy, the dependent.

Job indicates the appropriate response to these *ebyon* when he describes his personal identification with those in need:

> I was eyes to the blind,
> and feet to the lame.
> I was father to the poor (**ebyon**)
> and I searched out the cause of him
> whom I did not know (Job 29:15-16).

Job's response was the only possible response when we met a deaf and dumb stowaway. We had parked a borrowed jeep downtown after transporting some people back to Manila from a conference. It was late, but the crowds continued hustling and bustling. A boy in ragged clothes indicated he would watch our jeep for us and make sure that no one stole it. We nodded agreement, knowing that for many boys this was their only income.

On returning, we gave him a peso for his trouble. He signalled his thanks, but seemed strangely silent. He went and sat down again in the shop doorway.

I got into the driver's seat, but the compassion of Christ would not let me start the jeep. 'Do you think he's deaf?' I asked my companion, a social worker.

She nodded. I sat and thought. How could I return home to my luxury and leave one in such destitution.

'Let's go talk with him,' I called back, leaping out of the jeep and squatting beside him. I tried speaking, but he just nodded his head. Fortunately my companion had some training in sign language. Here is the sign language story he told:

'I came from Cebu (a city on an island south of Manila). I stowed away on a boat. It travelled three days and three nights. I arrived in Manila with three pesos in my pocket.'

The signs were accompanied with fear and hope. My friend translated them into English.

'Why did you leave home?' I asked.

'Why did you leave home?' she signalled.

He nodded and with great rapidity of hand action explained, 'They always used to laugh at me. My father used to beat me because I was deaf.'

She translated. I nodded.

'Where do you live?' she signalled.

His home was in a six-by-three-foot packing case, slotted in amongst the others by the river. He looked at me hopefully.

I knew a restaurant in the park that was staffed by people from a school for the deaf. We signalled to him that we would fetch him the next day and take him there.

The next day we collected him and from there found a school for the deaf run by some fine Catholic laymen, Some years later I heard of him successfully working as a chicken farmer.

This is not poverty caused by sin; it is poverty caused by natural calamity. It is of these poor that Jesus spoke when answering the query of John the Baptist ('Are you he who is to come, or shall we look for another?'):

> the blind receive their sight, the lame walk, lepers are cleansed, and the deaf hear . . . (Luke 11:3-4).

Jesus also describes them quoting Deuteronomy 15:11:

> For the poor (**ebyon**) will never cease out of the land, therefore I command you, 'You shall open wide your hand to your brother, to the needy (**ebyon**) and to the poor (**ani**) in the land.'

It is to these *ebyon* that God's kingdom brings healing and socio-economic uplift.

I'm too frail to work

'*Oy, Kumusta?*' (How are you?) 'How's your job-hunting going?' She smiled, embarrassed and replied, 'I can't take a job.'

'Oh, why is that?' She had studied in the same class as Coring, who was sitting typing for me at the plywood table of my kitchen-cum-office.

'I'm too weak. I cannot work five days a week, so I cannot take a job.' She looked away, staring sadly at the drawn-back sack that acted as a curtain.

I went to my room and wept. I felt something of the sorrow God must feel for such people. Who would rescue these poor?

Poverty is frailty and weakness. In Hebrew the root word is *dal*. This word is connected with the word *dallah*, the 'class of the poor'.

The Old Testament (2 Kings 24:14) describes the poorest in the land who were left behind during the exile to Babylon.

Jeremiah (5:4) tells us that these poor ones were looked down upon, while Job (20:19) tells us that they are easily crushed and abandoned, without the means to recover from loss or calamity.

These *dal* are blessed in the kingdom. In the song of Hannah we read:

He raises the frail poor (**dal**) from the dust,
He lifts the needy (**ebyon**) from the ash heap,
To make them sit with princes
And inherit a seat of honour (1 Samuel 2:8).

Husband of widows

Widows also fall into this category of those made poor by calamity.

Quietness stole softly over the lighted rooms beneath, replacing the cacophony of the sound of a thousand people crowded into the plywood homes I'd grown to love. The moon and the stars silhouetted the patchwork of old tyres holding down the roofs from typhoons. It was midnight, the hour for quiet prayer.

My heart ached for the situation of the widow next door. She had been kind to me. My prayers ranged over the houses of other widows. I thought of the rice they'd cooked that night for their children, some without fish, meat or vegetables.

I prayed, 'Lord, if perhaps I could marry all these widows I could meet their needs!' Quickly I thought to myself 'What a stupid prayer', so I added, 'But I can't do that!'

Suddenly, I realised, 'Lord, I don't have to for, if you are the Father of orphans, surely that makes you the Husband of widows! They are especially yours!'

I began to pray for ways to help these women. Who made the calamity of their poverty? They were poor through no sin of their own, nor even the sin of others. Their circumstances had simply happened. And so God takes responsibility for them:

The Lord watches over the sojourners,
He upholds the widow and the fatherless (Psalm 146:9).

We, too, are to incarnate his love amongst these *dallah*.

Children of sweat

Children, too, are important to Jesus. They also belong among the frail and the weak — the *dallah*. How can one help but love children? As I walked down the back paths into the community, I would hear all down the road *'Kuya Viv! Kuya Viv!'* (meaning 'Big brother Viv!'). Small children would laughingly greet me all the way until I reached my own house. Often we would play games together.

Yet ninety-two per cent of the children and eighty-seven per cent of the total population suffer from intestinal parasites. Sixty-nine per cent of Filipino children under six years of age are in various stages of protein calorie malnutrition. A further forty-five per cent of them have first degree malnutrition, meaning they are ten to twenty-four per cent below their standard weight.[6]

Indelibly lined in my mind is the memory of my friend, holding in her arms a little child with swollen stomach, spindly arms, swollen head. He was sick and retching constantly. She tried to comfort him while telling me that, when his father came home, she would get some money for him for medicine. I knew he had no money. On the mat slept five of the other eleven children.

There is a Tagalog phrase, *'anak-pawis'*, which means 'child of sweat', 'child of poverty'. John the Apostle said:

If anyone has the world's goods and sees his brother in need, yet closes his heart against him, how does God's love abide in him? (1 John 3:17).

Poverty is dispossession

There is yet another cause of poverty beyond the realm of personal sin and the calamities of life.

The cause of much poverty is oppression and exploitation. This is poverty caused by the sins of the rich, the leaders of a people or the oppression of another conquering nation. Two Hebrew words are related to this: *rush* and *ani*.

Rush means 'the dispossessed poor, the impoverished'. Such is the poverty of the tenant farmers forced off their lands to make way for the transnational sugar and banana plantations, or because of land reforms.

Proverbs 13:23 tells us:

The fallow ground of the poor yields much food, but it is swept away through injustice.

Many squatters come to Manila because their livelihoods have been swept away by injustices. The story of Tatalon itself is the story of injustice and dispossession. It all began with the oppression of the Spanish.

At one point the Spanish propagated a law regarding the need to file for titles to land. Since the peasants knew little Spanish, they were unaware of the law and unable to gain titles to their lands. Those families close to the Spaniards utilized the law for their own ends. This resulted in the land around Manila being owned in vast tracts by just a few families.

One of these families was that of J.M. Tuason. He owned the land now known as the Tatalon Estate. Dating back to the pre-war period, the Tatalon Estate's history was characterized by claims, counter-claims, controversies and court cases between J.M. Tuason and Co. and several other claimants.

Barely noticed in the thick of the ownership controversies was the steady growth of an unwanted population in Tatalon.

Social unrest began gripping the area, almost reaching boiling point in the late 1950s when Tuason and his administrator, Araneta, carried out mass ejectment and demolition on the basis of an 'authority to eject' issued by the courts.

I learned of the battles that raged when I sat one evening with Aling Cita, leader of the women:

'In those days Araneta came in with bulldozers to bulldoze down the squatter homes. We put them up the next night. Sometimes we surrounded the bulldozers. Some people lay down in front of them so they could not move. It was during that time that the old man up on the hill had his face beaten, so his lip became twisted and curled and his teeth were broken. He was one of the first people here — our leader. He was beaten by Araneta's henchmen.

'But through it all the community came together. As time went on, the National Housing Authority was able to buy the land from Araneta. Now the squatters can own their own land. I went to General Tobias myself and asked him to put in the water pumps. These are better days...'

Poverty is dispossession. This is essentially a passive phenomenon. It is the people being disinherited: first in the province, then in the city. God looks for an intercessor who will seek justice for these poor:

> But this is a people robbed and plundered... they have become a prey with none to rescue, a spoil with none to say 'restore!' (Isaiah 42:22).

White slavery

The dispossessed also include slaves. One week, Aling Ada had her daughter taken by a syndicate that enslaves girls in drugs and prostitution. These syndicates jail their girls in barred houses, force them into prostitution and, after a couple of years, not only physically but emotionally they're enslaved for life. It's called white slavery. She escaped a week later. One talks of darkest Africa, or General William Booth's 'In Darkest England'. The tourist belts in the Asian cities can rightly be called darkest Asia.

As slum statistics are unmentioned in the Year Books of Asian nations, so slavery is officially not spoken of. In the provinces, recruiters tempt girls with offers of good jobs in Manila. But upon reaching the city, they find themselves locked into these 'safe houses' from which there is no escape. Once forced into the trade, the desire and ability to escape such a lifestyle goes. Few get out.[7]

Others are sold by employment agencies to men in the Middle East, Italy, Japan, Hong Kong and elsewhere, often under the guise of being waitresses or housegirls.

Bangkok's population, for example, of 8.3 million includes a small army of 60,000 women, mostly prostitutes, working out of 350 go-go bars, 130 massage parlours and 100 dance halls.

The women who make the sex business successful in Bangkok see few profits for themselves. Travel agents skin off fifty per cent of the take, bars and brothels pocketing most of the remainder, with varying cuts from that share for the B-girls.

'We are down to our last resource,' says Karina David, a professor of community development at the University of the Philippines. 'Once you sell your women and debase your culture, there is not much left.'[8]

Amos pronounces God's judgement on a nation for the same sin:

> Because they sell the righteous for silver and the needy for a pair of shoes, they that trample the head of the poor into the dust of the earth and turn aside the way of the afflicted (Amos 2:6-7).

God looks for women of commitment who would both give their lives to rescuing these girls and to effecting changes in the law to break the horrendous sale of flesh that parades itself under the name of tourism. It is a dangerous task. Two Japanese friends who tried to combat it at a government level were threatened so often they gave up. Yet Proverbs 31:9 tells us to 'open your mouth, judge righteously, maintain the rights of the poor and needy'.

Perhaps we are more concerned with make-up and beauty than with the rescue of slaves in the context of possibly being murdered! God looks for women who know that God is our protector, as he was for Amy Carmichael and her band of women rescuing temple prostitutes in India.

Who are the blessed poor?

The fifth Hebrew word used in the Old Testament is *ani* and its derivative *anaw*, which is the word Jesus used when he talks of the blessed poor.

The root word means to bring low, to afflict, to ravish, to violate or force and is used for a whole range of exercises in domination such as when the people of Israel were afflicted by their taskmasters in Egypt (Exodus 1:11-12). It was used also to denote the response of humble dependence on God to such oppression (Job 34:28; Psalms 34:6). The *ani* is one who is bowed down under pressure, one occupying a lowly position, one who finds himself in a dependent relationship. It means 'the humble poor of Yahweh' or 'God's poor ones'.

The *ani* are not contrasted with the rich, but with the men of violence, the oppressors who 'turn aside justice from them' (Amos

2:7), who rob the poor of their right by making unjust laws and publishing burdensome decrees (Isaiah 10:1-2). Much of the poverty of the Third World countries can be attributed to such causes. Several centuries of such iniquitous decrees by both the Spanish and the rich 400 families that rule the Philippines have resulted in a society oppressed, afflicted and impoverished.

These blessed poor, then, include the needy (*ebyon*) and the frail (*dal*), the dispossessed (*rush*) and those who lack (*chaser*). But within these categories, also, underlying them, is poverty caused by the ruthlessness of the powerful, who both deny their rights and do not respond to their calamities.

Is poverty blessed?
No! God rebels against this poverty, for it destroys his whole creation. Nowhere in the Bible is poverty an ideal, as it is with the later mystics. Nowhere is poverty glorified or romanticised. The fact that the poor are sometimes, and with increasing frequency in the scriptures, called righteous is not so much to their own credit. They are righteous because their oppressors are so terribly unrighteous. The poor are therefore righteous *in comparison* with the oppressor who withholds their rights.

Nor are the poor blessed because of their material lack or their economic class. This would ignore salvation by grace and imply, with the Marxists and Liberation theologians, that salvation is by economic and sociological status. Poverty is not blessed, but the poor are — those poor who become *disciples*. For the Beatitudes were spoken to Christ's *disciples*. These poor were truly 'the poor of Yahweh'. Because of their poverty, they trusted in God in a spirit of dependence. Matthew 5:3 ('Blessed are the poor in spirit') and Luke 6:20 ('Blessed are you poor') are both expressions of this idea.

The solution: discipleship
In summary we may split the causes of poverty into three main categories: poverty caused by personal sin (*chaser*); poverty caused by calamity (*ebyon* and *dal*); and poverty caused by oppression (*ani, anaw* and *rush*).

Discipleship changes the poverty caused by personal sin. Membership in God's kingdom brings love, releases guilt, heals bitterness and breaks the power of drunkenness, immorality and gambling. It results in a new motivation for work. Our response to such poverty must be to live amongst these poor and preach the gospel by deed and by word. (This is the theme of chapter 9.)

Discipleship changes the poverty of the frail and the weak, for true disciples will aid the widows and orphans, welcome the stranger and the refugee and help the destitute. God's power can heal the blind and the deaf. Our response to such poverty is relief, economic projects, and protection of the weak. (This is the theme of chapter 10.)

Discipleship also changes poverty caused by oppression, injustice and exploitation. Disciples defend these oppressed poor by bringing justice. (This is the theme of chapter 11.)

In the context of poverty, the gospel is a gospel both of judgement and of mercy. To the rich and oppressor it is a message of judgement and woe, requiring repentance. As Jesus says:

> Woe to you that are rich, for you have received your consolation. Woe to you that are full now, for you shall hunger. Woe to you that laugh now, for you shall mourn and weep (Luke 6:23-26).

But to the poor the gospel is a message of uplift, if they would but repent and believe:

'Come to me, all who labour and are heavy laden and I will give you rest...' (Matthew 12:28).

To the poor the gospel is a message of blessing, both now and in the future:

> Blessed are you poor, for yours **is** the kingdom of God. Blessed are you that hunger now, for you **shall** be satisfied. Blessed are you that weep now, for you **shall** laugh (Luke 6:20-21).

For the poor receive the kingdom gladly now. There will come a day when all oppression will cease and all the unjust receive their dues. On that day the poor will laugh and leap for joy, for each will have his mansion. There will be no more pain, no more sorrow, no more tears!

Blessed are you poor, for yours is — and shall be — the kingdom of God!

Footnotes on chapter 3

1. For a fuller analysis, see Harvey L. Perkins, *The Poor and Oppressed: The Focus of Christian Participation in Human Development*, Colleagues in Development; Bible Study Series, Singapore, Christian Conference of Asia (mimeo-series, 1977 to present). Also, Julio de Sta Ana, *Good News to the Poor*, Geneva, World Council of Churches, 1977.

2. Conrad Boerma, *'Rich Man, Poor Man — and The Bible'*, SCM, London 1979. Chapters 2 and 3 have a brief summary of the themes in the Bible related to poverty including a brief contrast between *ptochos*, the beggar, and *penes*, the industrious poor man.

3. F. Landa Jocano, *Slum as a Way of Life*, University of the Philippines Press, Quezon City, 1975, p 31

4. Figure from a description of the Tatalon Estate Zonal Improvement Project, furnished by the National Housing Authority, Quezon City.

5. Donald Denise Decaesstecker, *Impoverished Urban Filipino Families*, UST Press, Manila, 1978, p 126, an in-depth study of the structure and problems of impoverished slum families in one of Manila's slums.

6. Tom Steers, *Understanding the Philippines*, Navigator Orientation Manual

7. F. Landa Jocano, *op. cit.*, chapter IX, 'Deviant Females'

8. Quoted in 'An Ironic Furor about Photographs', *Newsweek Magazine*, May 31, 1982, p 24. An article on the growing sex trade in Manila. See also 'Lust City in the Far East', *Time Magazine*, May 10, 1982, p 29, for a description of a similar problem in Bangkok.

4
Living as a Poor Man
LEARNING TO IDENTIFY

TWO THOUSAND YEARS AGO a grain of wheat fell from the sower's hand, from heaven to earth. The God of eternity now inhabited humility in the cry of a child, in the frame of a manger, in the tramp of sandalled feet.

But the symphony the angels sang at Jesus' birth was tinged by the melancholy of poverty. For in coming from heaven to earth, the grain did not remain at surface level amongst the unrealities of the rich and the haughty. He buried himself in the depths of humanity. And those depths have been weighted against the labouring poor for thousands of years.

The prophet Isaiah, 600 years earlier, had declared that God has two homes:

> For thus says the high and lofty one who inhabits **eternity** whose name is holy:
> I dwell in the high and holy place,
> And also with him who is of a **contrite and lowly** spirit
> (Isaiah 57:15)

Two homes, two addresses: eternity and poverty.

The language of the poor
My real training in the knowledge of the God who dwells amongst the poor (i.e. in theology) had begun during language study by the flicker of a kerosene lamp as I was served by *Ate* Luz, daughter of Ka Emilio (*Ate* meaning big sister). Here I began to learn the heart-beat, the soul, the language of the poor.

I looked out across the nipa thatch to the sky. The scene had all the drama of a traditional missionary movie scene, but beneath this harmony lay that same melancholy of suffering in which Jesus dwelt. Luz and Emy, her husband, ran out of food each twentieth of the month. Over a period of time we worked out a way to provide for the family by my paying the equivalent of my food costs for Ate Luz's cooking. Initially, in the style of Filipino hospitality, they gave me too much food until I explained that I should live on what they lived on — though I requested them to add some extra meat to maintain my vitamin B level. They improved their own food with the money earned by Ate Luz. (I never did learn what their former level was!)

It is in the language of these poor that Jesus spoke. His Beatitudes, his Sermon on the Mount, made no sense to the rich of his day, just as they make little sense today to the majority of 20th century middle-class Christians.

Perhaps he learned it from his mother. Mary, in her Magnificat before Jesus' birth, tells how the Lord 'has regarded the low estate of his handmaiden' and speaks prophetically of him 'filling the hungry with good things, but sending the rich empty away' (Luke 1:48 and 53). These are a poor woman's words, just as Jesus' instruction to 'give to everyone who asks you' (Luke 6:39) is a saying of the poor, an expression not found in rich men's vocabulary. He was one of the poor and so he used their words, their phraseology. 'The poor people heard him gladly' (Mark 12:36).

Metamorphosis

In the process of entering God's being, we also enter fully into true manliness (or femininity) and into the complete nature of our humanity, our society and culture. For he set us a pattern when he 'became a man and dwelt amongst us, full of grace and truth and we have beheld his glory' (John 1:14).

Being 'full of grace' means that Jesus fully entered in or fully mastered the intricacies of our cultural forms. He spent thirty years learning Aramaic and Jewish culture.

Being 'full of truth' means there are elements in his life that supercede all cultures, that refuse to adapt to the evil in any culture. We have 'beheld his glory' as he expressed God's culture through the thought-forms and actions of the Jewish soul.

Many people think of cultural change as adjusting to heat (30°) or humidity (98.5%), living on a diet of fish and rice, being called an *Americano*, having to adapt to the daily pattern of siestas, travelling in a jeepney, eating at a *carinderia* (a snack shop), or bargaining for a shirt.

These are initial exposures. For example, my first real taste of culture shock was when I planned for a day of sports for the Bible study leaders from the Bible school. With Kiwi ruggedness we played volleyball all morning and planned to play soccer all afternoon. At one o'clock everyone curled up for a sleep! Later on I was to learn of siestas. Then it began to rain, so everyone decided to go home! I did not know how to take this. Later I learned that poor people cannot afford to get wet, for their diet and lifestyle give little resistance against sickness. I felt an absolute failure.

These things are initial adjustments, involving some degree of culture stress which, if it is beyond our emotional capacity, could result in culture shock. But these experiences are fun and relatively easy to comprehend compared with the issues of cultural change.

Cultural change is primarily a matter of *inner* changes: change not at the level of external behaviour (important though this is in becoming 'full of grace'), but at the level of our inner emotional responses. Knowledge, study, wisdom, experience and language are all necessary. It is here that dying to self is critical.

But the understanding of values, even emotional adaptation, is insufficient for a servant of God. We cannot simply replace our Western culture with Filipino culture. Rather we must evaluate *both* cultures against biblical values — we must move from a Western expression of biblical character to a Filipino expression. No culture is absolute. Only the scriptures are. The Bible judges all cultures.

One can spend days contrasting the culture of New Zealand — 'the passionless people' as one author calls us — with Filipino culture, certainly not lacking in passion. Intellectual understanding comes slowly. Change in one's emotional responses comes even more so, as one moves from individualism to group-centredness; from the Kiwi authoritarian, structure-oriented leadership model to Filipino consensus decision-making; from a male-dominated society to a matriarchal society; from frugality to a celebrating lifestyle; from an egalitarian society (all men are equal) to a traditionally status-oriented society; from achievement-orientation to people-orientation.

How do you rebuke in a society that knows little direct rebuke? What is my status, where status is based on position, wealth, power, age, good looks and whiteness of face, whereas in New Zealand status is almost entirely related to achievements.

Lessons in child-raising

In living with Ka Emilio, I was in a perfect situation to observe two areas: child-raising patterns (the basis of indigenous training concepts) and family life (the basis of indigenous group structures, social relationships and value systems).

One interesting feature of child-raising patterns are that control and discipline are not maintained by *punishment* for violation of principles, but rather by the *presence* of the mother (or aunt, or older sister), who constantly limits and moulds the child's behaviour according to the responses of people around.

One evening I was sitting at the table eating supper. Emy was dramatizing his courtship for me. Little Alma, three years old, was running around. *'Huwag kang malikot,'* Ate Luz admonished the small boy. This means 'Don't run around' and also 'Don't be naughty'. To be too active is to be naughty: an active child is difficult to control.

Shame is the critical element. Often I would hear *'Baka, magalit si Viv'* (Watch out, Viv might get angry) as a way of shaming a child into obedience. To make someone angry is a great sin.

Later in life, the same social mechanisms function in the development of ministry and eldership teams: a constant sensitivity to the group; a moulding of each other little by little; little direct rebuke; group controls exercised by the mechanism of 'shaming' a group member if he oversteps the mark. Groups are very conscious of what onlookers think of the group as a whole, lest they be shamed.

Shock!

Culture shock occurs when cultural stress is beyond our capacity to cope, causing us to react emotionally and irrationally, and revert to the immature reactions of childhood. In a sense you must become a child again — see yourself as a child learning the simplest things of life. Culture shock is the result of tension between our prior experience and our current status. Our 'ego' is suddenly undermined.

Culture shock is the result of failure added to failure: Failure in bargaining, failure in giving due respect to an official, failure in language, failure in ministry.

One morning I jotted: 'Life here is full of the failure of cultural adjustment. Failure in saying the right thing, doing the right thing, thinking the right thing. But only in failure comes success. Only in death is life, only in pressing into further failure comes the metamorphosis of cultural adaptation. That's the joy of being a missionary. That is the thrill of mission: walking into death in order to find life — and the knowledge of the One who conquered death.'

The culture stress of those months of language study amongst the poor of Lipa City had many components. Knowing of no clear directions, I had to carve out new models of ministry. Knowing of no group, no organization from which to recruit others to work with the urban poor, I had to raise up co-labourers. I was not used to having no team around me and missed the thrust and parry of activity that had been my lifestyle for years. The uncertainties of ever mastering the language, of ever doing anything significant, at times would overwhelm me, only to be rolled back by meditation on such scriptures as 'Wait for the Lord, be strong and let your heart take courage'.

And there is stress relating to other missionaries. The most difficult cultural adjustments were not to Filipino culture but to American. I think it would be true to say that most Kiwis (the nickname for New Zealanders) grow up with an antipathy to American culture for its apparent arrogance. The same appears to be true of most Australian and British people. We grow with a deep nationalism that identifies our egalitarian culture ('she'll be right') as superior to that of American capitalism and its 'man-is-a-machine' administration systems. Many times I had to bring these prejudices before God in repentance. But love covers a multitude of sins. Missionaries of different races need to walk in forgiving love and learn to humbly let others assume that their culture is better than ours.

Such are the quirks of our fallen nature that I had to consciously seek the positive aspects of other cultures. From our British heritage I have learned the importance of being a scholar and a gentleman; from our American brethren I have learned the importance of productivity and achievement; from our Kiwi background how to take life as it comes and to pioneer; from Filipino culture I have learned how to enjoy life and people.

In time one comes to a degree of cultural sensitivity. Many missionaries looking back on those first years wish they had taken more time for study of the surrounding culture. However, the demands of people, leadership roles and our own personal expectations promote impatience, and a jettisoning of the ideal of concentration on culture and language learning needed to become a worthy servant of God, acceptable to him and to the people.

It is a wise 'grain' that takes the full time of winter to die — full time needed to read, study, think, experiment and internalise the life of the new culture into which it is being planted.

Finally, there come long periods when one knows one is entering into the soul of the people — beginning to speak their soul language and know a little of their soul music. Such periods are rudely broken by the inbuilt values in any culture which reject foreigners. This rejection prevents full integration and reminds us that we are strangers and exiles in this world, looking forward to a more permanent dwelling. Such intermittent rejection should also remind us that we will never fully understand another culture — that we are guests in another's 'house' and must accept that limitation.

Language study

In becoming man, Jesus took the time to learn our language, to learn our heartbeat. He came walking softly, speaking on our terms in our language.

Initially, language study increases stress by its very monotony, by its constant failure, failure, failure and by forcing one out to talk with people one does not understand. But as time goes on, the increasing facility for communication provides warmth, laughter and love. The process of studying the language leads one in a series of supervised cultural learning experiences.

Language study is an emotional life. An apple and taped vocabulary at 5 a.m., chatter with the little boy next door about everything under the sun, five hours of tutoring, a last listen to the tape before one sleeps, and tomorrow and tomorrow... until March next year. It is a droning air-conditioner punctuated by the humdrum repetition of a phrase, a phrase, a phrase — and four dead-pan, weary faces.

Each day begins with a drama. Then mastery of the dialogue and grammar, rote-memorizing of the phrases and finally heading out to practice on friends. In the middle is a break for a snack or a game of table tennis.

By the end of the morning, one's classmates are mentally exhausted. We fail and fail again at language. But there's the thrill in daily becoming more skilled with words, of talking to people, of being able to understand a TV program, of preaching for the first time in Tagalog. Finally freedom begins to come, and that same exultant feeling we had when we first learned to whistle, or swim, or tie our shoelaces.

My first sermon in Tagalog was a message on love. It was a beautiful experience to learn some of the deepest Tagalog words about the soul. The next sermon was a message on the cross and the conditions of discipleship.

And there are dangers! In one area where I travelled there is a word which means that, should a single man look over his shoulder upon leaving a house, he is proposing courtship. I wonder how many thought I proposed during that trip!

And there is humour! I recall my first day in Tatalon. I had been looking for the pump. *'Nasaan ang bomba?' (Where is the bomba*?), I inquired of a group of ladies. There was silence, then a round of hilarious laughter. I thought *bomba* meant pump. It means a 'sexy' movie star! The ladies still joked with me about it years later.

Executive footwasher

But Jesus not only became fully human, learning our language and ways: he not only dwelt amongst the poor. He chose something deeper — an inner dependence of spirit, an inner humility:

> For though he was in the form of God,
> [he] did not count equality with God
> a thing to be grasped,
> but emptied himself,
> taking the form of a servant,
> being born in the likeness of man.
> And being found in human form
> he humbled himself
> and became obedient unto death
> even death on a cross . . . (Philippians 2:5-8).

How easy to live as a poor man; how hard to be a poor man's servant! How easy is external poverty; how hard is poverty of the spirit! External identification must always be matched by inner humility.

The executive sits behind his expensive desk, swinging quietly in his leather chair as the conversation progresses, file tray in, file tray out, dictaphone, telephone, secretary's clickety-clack, harbour view, air-conditioned room. Perhaps it's you or is it me? Quietly, in control of his world.

Secure! Powerful! Wealthy! Proud!

For pride feeds on security, pride feeds on wealth, pride feeds on control and success. My training as an engineer, plus my early training as a mission executive, taught me to control, taught me the paths to power, success and efficiency — and taught me pride.

How subtle that pride! These poor — Emy, Luz, Ka Emilio — wished to honour me as a Westerner as I ate with them. They wished that I not do my share of the physical labour of fetching water. I had to deliberately work hard at choosing the lowest place and the most difficult jobs.

I watched one missionary friend who came to believe that the honour given him by Filipino friends was his rightful heritage, that he was indeed receiving just honour. We must never believe the lie that says we are better than another because we have a white face or a fat wallet. We must constantly renounce such flattery. The very heart of identification is the communication to another that he, or she, too, is a person of equal worth. We need to actively choose the apparently inefficient way, even to sidestep the seemingly important people, that we might honour the nobodies! Such was Jesus' style.

People's respect and honour must not stem from my white skin and wealth. It must come from the recognition of the Lord within me, that same Lord who:

> Knowing that he had come from and was going to God, rose from supper, laid aside his garments and girded himself with a towel. Then he poured water into a basin and began to wash the disciples' feet and to wipe them with the towel with which he was girded! (John 13:3-5).

I heard on the news of one of the world's great religious leaders washing the feet of twelve old men. For this menial task he used a pure gold basin! The princes of the church, the men of power, riches and authority, the international congress on this or that have some small influence on the kingdom. But servants? They are God's strategy.

In dying to ourselves, respect will not come because of a powerful position. It will be because of the power of Christ. That power comes through small acts of humility — the choosing of the lesser place, the less thankful tasks.

Andrew Murray defines humility as: 'perfect quietness of heart; it is never sore or irritated or disappointed. It is to expect nothing, to wonder at nothing that is done to me, to be at rest when nobody praises me and when I am blamed and despised.'

Opposition from missionary friends helped reinforce my commitment to humility. A very wise evangelist friend visited me in Ka Emilio's house and over breakfast advised me not to be critical of those who chose a richer lifestyle, since God is impartial and so works mainly with the rich. (This was not his intention, but this was the outworking of his theology!) I was tired of the old arguments, so kept my peace. He pointed out that the inefficiency of a lifestyle of poverty would hinder my ministry.

Yet efficiency, too, is a part of us as Westerners that must die if the gospel be preached to the poor. The choice of seeming *inefficiency* is a choice which ultimately brings *effectiveness*. By neglecting our customary patterns of effectiveness, we find our Lord's patterns beginning to manifest themselves — the patterns of humility, of becoming fully human, of identification. I could only continue in the belief that poverty and humility are both prerequisites to real spiritual power and to a successful ministry. I wrote:

> I easily get wiped out and discouraged unless each day I get that time with God, going over every attitude, meditating on each detail of life and praying over each step forward. If I do not spend that time, I will never have the dependence on God and humility to survive emotionally in this place, nor can God advance his kingdom.

During this time of meditating on these issues and of rejecting traditional mission patterns, the life of St Francis Xavier and Francis of Assisi were strong encouragements. For Xavier, poverty was the protection for the religious leader against deterioration into a life of comfort. It secured him from the desire for possessions to which so many monasteries had succumbed. Both Xavier and Assisi saw poverty as essentially apostolic — it enabled them to serve more freely, to evangelize more effectively.

For Francis of Assisi poverty was his 'bride', his chosen 'lady'. Xavier too loved poverty dearly. He replaced the Franciscan image of 'bride' by that of 'mother'.

It was encouraging also to note how Xavier and his companions learned poverty by experimentation, by going with nothing on ministry trips. At times they stored nothing; at times (such as in foreign lands) they took provisions. It encouraged me to persevere.[1]

A renewed passion for the inner mastery of my conditions

began to develop. I was thankful for the seven years of rugged Navigator training in the discipline of thought, developed through Scripture memorization and intensive Bible study. Now the choice of poverty was compelling me to a new level of discipline — the disciplines Jesus gave us in the Sermon on the Mount, the disciplines of spirit. I wrote to a friend:

The sincerity of our desire to win the world to Christ is measured by the yardstick of self-conquest. Men and women back home ought first to direct their zeal to the conquest of their own relationships, possessions and delights by the kingdom. You cannot wage war in a dark land, on a dark devil unless the war is first directed against egotism and self-love. For the man of God works frequently from a bed of sickness, in the midst of loneliness and bitterness, and in God we must conquer with joy.

We must expect and delight to share in the sufferings of Christ. Xavier taught that 'failing such a disposition, enthusiasm itself fails. The apostle cannot discharge the rigorous and exacting duties of his office if he becomes embittered by the thought that, at forty, he will be past his prime, by the loneliness of his wanderings, by the frequent 'you are aware that all who are in Asia have deserted me' or 'at the first no one stood to my defence.'

To the Christian, suffering is a delight, for it causes him so much more to become complete. External hardship leads to inner strength. External ease leads to flabbiness of soul.

We are to 'train ourselves in godliness'. Paul says, speaking figuratively, that 'I pommel my body and subdue it, lest after preaching to others I myself should be disqualified.' This joy, this ability to face suffering and utilize it for good, is the result of hard discipline in training our minds in small things.

There can be little success here without the daily memorizing of the word of God until hundreds and indeed thousands of verses control our thinking. I can well remember several godly men, about whose lives I have noticed an unusually toughened holiness. They were men of the memorized word, men of holy mind.

There were other encouragements. I read of Archbishop Dom Halder Camara of Recife, who turned his bishop's palace into a social services centre and went to live amongst the poor of the *favelos* (slums) of Latin America.

Time, truth and the heightened sensitivity to God caused by poverty worked to illuminate the calling God was placing upon my life. It was a call to demonstrate by word and deed an acceptable missionary lifestyle, a lifestyle of preaching the gospel to the poor, a desire to prophesy by action and by deed against the soul-destroying affluence of my church and country in the hope of his leading my own nation back to himself through economic repentance.

Along with the inner struggles grew an inner certainty, a knowledge of standing for a central truth that the Lord was speaking to the church. Also came the knowledge that I was at the critical point of need, where the social, economic and spiritual battle was being fought. And a growing sense that God would raise up a band of Filipinos to meet that need. A growing sense also, even at this point, that he would lead out a band of men and women from my own country to work amongst the poor. I began to think through the basis for a new missions structure from the suburbs of the West to the slums of the East.

Boxed in by humanity

Imitatio Cristi is an old phrase of the church that describes this life of identification with the poor, of incarnating Christ. The choice of such a life leads one deep into the very nature of Jesus' deity.

Jesus identified himself with the poor. But he never was *identical*. Though he could classify himself as a poor man, as one of the *anaw*, he was always God. He had two natures.

The white Western missionary has a similar duality of nature. No matter how simply one lives, one is always rich. We have travelled. We have a hundred rich friends. We are educated. We have white faces and long, Roman noses!

Becoming poor amongst the poor involves recognizing this duality; it is not becoming hopeless amongst the hopeless. It is, rather, involvement in the poor man's sufferings and lifestyle to both show that in Jesus alone is hope and to bring the riches of rich friends, the resources of wealth and education and power to bear on the felt and real points of need of the poor.

Jesus' incarnation was not that of becoming a malnourished beggar, but becoming *fully human* in the context of inhumanity. Identification is not destitution, but demonstrating by actions and revealing by deeds of spiritual power, by miracles and deeds of love, the fullness of Christ's deity in the midst of depravity.

We need beware of overemphasizing Jesus' poverty. Though he became poor, he ate daily, he had a finely woven robe, he grew up with a skilled trade as a *tekton* (a cross between a carpenter, cabinet maker and stone mason — a skilled job, perhaps equivalent today to that of an engineer or architect). He loved to celebrate and freely went to rich men's houses. He and the twelve gave to a class of poor yet poorer than themselves. Though at times, like Paul, we may choose a greater life of poverty and suffering for the gospel, we need to avoid the extremes of the ascetic poverty of Xavier and Assissi. We need to know the limitations of our chosen poverty.

The fear of economic insecurity

And the choice of such poverty raised another fear. Having read a hundred books on poverty, I knew that the poor will get poorer, that the disparity between the rich, military-political establishments in the world and the common people will increase as time goes on. I knew that those able to function in a computer technology will be able to continually amass more and more, while the poor may make small gains but ultimately the majority will fall back into the morass. And I was afraid.

I was afraid because the choice of poverty seems more costly than it would have been in Jesus' day. It is one thing to voluntarily choose a poverty from which I can move. But, if I do not develop the computer-age skills for which my engineering training prepared me, I may lose my options. I may become one of the *involuntary poor*.

Rather than identify, I'd like to hang on to both worlds — to become bicultural. And indeed that's the life I have ended up living — that of a poor rich man. I've chosen to maintain my skills in one world for use when needed, while living in the other world of poverty the majority of the time. So too, the Son of God moved from the realm of infinite riches to his life of poverty. So, too, we find St Francis Xavier, when confronted by the intransigence of the *Bonzes* of Japan, dressing up in all his glory as a *Papal Nuncio* and visiting them in state. His reason? To gain freedom to work amongst the poorest! And St Francis of Assissi in his poverty drew on his status as one of the sons of the rich to unite the rich and poor in his own divided city of Assissi.

The problem is the motivation behind one's bicultural lifestyle. For fear is the complete antithesis of Jesus' command to simplicity:

Therefore I tell you, do not be anxious about your life, what you shall eat, nor about your body, what you shall put on. Fear not little flock, for it is your Father's good pleasure to give you the kingdom. Sell your possessions, and give alms. . . (Luke 12:22, 32 and 33).

To help this Asian parish of over 150,000,000 poor, it is reasonable for one to choose to oscillate back into another lifestyle at times. This, however, must not be for personal protection lest we shrink back from the high calling of the poor Master to this life of external poverty and inner humility. Rather it must be always for the sake of these poor. And in all this he promises to provide for our needs.

In keeping this balance, let us not lose sight of the fact that the poor people loved Jesus who was all-powerful God. For he was approachable, one of them. He preached their stories and was loved by their children. His jokes were theirs — his eating and drinking, his dress and manners.

'Come and see,' he said to those who first knew of his mission. They must have marvelled at this simple Messiah. Being God, he chose to limit himself. His chosen humanity restricted him to a particular place, time, language, culture and circle of friends.

Our humanity limits us similarly. This is not always by choice, but by its very weakness. At one stage I made a list of these limitations:

(a) Limited by privacy; the need for room and time to study, to pray, to sleep.

I remember the first time I slept in the same bed with another co-worker. I did not sleep all night! For people who grow up sleeping on the same mat with their family, it is natural to share a bed. Indeed, it is strange to most Filipinos that a Westerner should wish to sleep in a private bedroom.

Fortunately as a university student I had learned to study in the midst of all sorts of noise and people. But at the same time every 'monk' needs his own cell for prayer and study.

(b) Limited by food needs.

Each day Ate Luz would boil my water, since my stomach had no resistance to amoeba, fungus, worms or bacteria. Even so, because it is hard to boil water on a wood fire, I soon contracted all four.

Having grown up on meat, I could ill afford to live on the staple diet of fish and rice, so we worked out an arrangement whereby I would eat some meat each day.

(c) Limited by my intellectual need for time to think.

For I am not only called to the poor. I am called to lead men and women. And such leadership requires mastery of complex issues. Much of my motivation to pioneer comes from the exploration of ideas, of theology.

(d) Limited by my emotional need for time out of this poverty
    to cope with culture shock.

One weekend a month I would return to Manila to fetch my mail and to enjoy some company with some other missionaries. Often I would watch a good British movie or a TV program so as to throw my mind back into Western culture.

(e) Limited by my achievement needs, built up through years of
    living and mastering an achievement-oriented culture.

(f) Limited by my needs to interface with my own culture
    through correspondence and typing.

(g) Limited by my own quietness, my seriousness, and
    directness.

At times I found I needed to retreat inside myself, away from the exuberance and display of emotions that make Filipinos such a fun-loving people.

Which Jesus?

A further complicating factor in the *Imitatio Cristi*, the lifestyle of imitating Christ, is that Jesus had several lifestyles.

He lived in a stable home and had a stable childhood. There was a long time of maturing, training and working. There were also times of withdrawal, times of mission, times of ministry.

The missionary in the slum also needs to be a quick-change artist from one lifestyle to another — within the same day being a poor man labouring in the slums, a successful missionary interacting with rich donors, an evangelist preaching to sinners and a mystic taking time out to be alone with God.

The simple result of many months of musing was the conclusion that I could call individuals, or couples without children, to live amongst the urban poor, provided they had:
* a good toilet
* control on cooking food
* control on boiling water
* a day of rest outside the slums each week
* a companion.

But what about those with children? Could they not have an effective ministry to the poor?

There is no simple answer. Raising children in the midst of poverty is a difficult task. To work from outside a community is a difficult, perhaps impossible task, yet could prove effective. John Wesley in his ministry succeeded by living outside the communities to whom he preached. Those with support roles, such as administration or the development of economic projects, could certainly do so from the outside of the slum communities.

Even those living within the slum communities will spend much time out of the communities working as middle-class or rich men and women in assisting the people to obtain justice, political assistance or economic aid, besides the time needed for rest, retreat or sickness.

Perhaps the critical issue is the heart commitment of a couple to identification with the poor. Where there is a will, there is a way!

Next steps

It was time for the Lord to teach the next step. I came back under orders to a friend's middle-class Manila home, sick with some amoeba. The doctor, an old man, prescribed the wrong medicine, affecting my heart and leaving me in bed for two months. I changed doctors, but by that time my liver was affected.

Language study was continued in Manila, as I regained health.

At the same time I was asked to draw together the leadership of some Bible studies for professionals and office workers throughout Manila. I made the mistake of accepting, despite my being in the middle of language study. The Lord rebuked me, pointing out that the decision would end in catastrophe, not only for my language study but also because it was a deviation from my clear calling to the poor. In mission, one needs always to be open to sense God's leading through leadership and through the body. In this case it was not his leading I was hearing. It was my own fear of rejection.

But God used this experience for good. The task of drawing the professionals together was used to teach me the deeper components of various disciple-making models that were emerging in the Filipino church. At the same time I was able to develop a theology of holistic discipleship, relating it to a biblical theology of poverty, of development and of economics. From the theology, a strategy of ministry emerged.

These were prerequisites for a ministry to the squatters.

Footnote on chapter 4

1. The best motivational books I have found on these men are Paul Sabatier, *Life of St Francis of Assissi*, Hodder and Stoughton, London, 1907.

Xavier Leon Dujour, S.J., tr. from French by Fr Henry Pascual Oiz, S.J., *Saint Francis Xavier, The Mystical Progress of the Apostle*, St Paul Press Training School, Bandra, Bombay, 1976.

5

Paved with Good Intentions
INADEQUATE CONCEPTS OF DISCIPLESHIP

THE DESTINY OF THIS WORLD is determined by those who have captured the heartbeat of the Master and whose hearts begin to beat with his love and justice.

History is replete with men and women who have given their lives singlemindedly to the task of transferring the character of the Master from one generation of new believers to the next, who have given their lives to establishing movements of disciples of the Master.

This process of multiplying disciples began with him. It was central to all he did. In his final prayer before he was taken to the cross he told his Father, 'I have accomplished the work which thou gavest me to do.'

He then reiterated these accomplishments. They were chiselled into the lives of twelve men: 'I have given *them* thy words... *they* have believed... I am praying for *them*... I have guarded *them*... for *their* sake I consecrate myself...' (John 17:4-19).

From these twelve came the first discipling movement. To them Jesus commanded, 'You go now, and make disciples.' The passion for a lifestyle of disciple-making was *his* passion.

I had grown up with such a close-knit band of men and women, people with a demanding dream. We had a drive and zeal for one thing: to make disciples and thus to bring a world to the knowledge of our Lord. We were confident of our plan, sure of our steps, fully committed to our methodology. There were a score of us now scattered in countries across the globe.

But in order to reach the poor God decided to shatter that demanding dream, that passion, that zeal and then remake it after his own model. He did it very simply through a destitute woman.

'Brod, pahingi?'

She came to me after I had stopped for some hours of prayer in a beautiful Catholic chapel.

Often I went there. It was one place where I could be reasonably alone from the ever-probing, demanding, laughing eyes of Manila's crowds. The walls were open, looking out on to green grass and great old trees — a pleasant sight in a city of dust and concrete.

The hours of quiet had left me feeling religious, holy, together again, ready for another week of action. I walked beneath the restful trees towards the bus stop.

'Brod... brod!'

I felt the voice, rather than heard it.

'Brod, brod!' I looked behind me and a shudder ran through me, though my body betrayed nothing. Never had I seen such an ugly face. I felt ashamed at my response. She came hesitatingly to me and I waited for her request. There must be a request.

'Brod, brod, pahingi twenty pesos!' (Brother, brother, please give me twenty pesos!). She spoke softly, urgently, uncertainly, unlike the professional, brazen beggars. She was hopelessly ashamed. The face was pock-marked all over. Not the usual beautiful honey brown, but the colour of a pink powder puff, covered in protusions and hollows. The little child on her hip was obviously very sick. Revulsion checked, my attitude changed to one of compassion. But shock caused me to stand and stare.

A wild light in her eyes indicated desperation had overtaken shame and she pressed her advantage, 'Brod, pahingi, fifty pesos.' She reached out to grasp my arm. I inwardly cowed back. Again I was overwhelmed with compassion.

'Bakit, mare? Ang bang problema?' (Why mother, what's your problem?), I asked, knowing as I asked that the humiliation she would suffer answering would require me to give.

Her child would be hospitalized. She herself was nearing death. She was afraid to die while he was there.

As I listened and looked at her, it flashed through my mind that in my wallet I had one hundred pesos. In my pocket I had two. Suddenly her boldness overcame all her reserve.

'Brod, pahingi one hundred pesos!' I thought of lunch and my busfare. Lunch was not that important anymore. I gave her the one hundred pesos.

She left as softly and as quickly as she had come, blowing my life to pieces, embarrassed and murmering, 'God bless you.'

For days I travelled across Manila attending to the myriad of jobs that go to making up a ministry, oblivious to the people, the city and the smells.

A lifetime's battle was going on within. Years of my life teaching a 'spiritual' concept of discipleship were face-to-face with a repulsive woman, a child and her haunting pleas. And I could not cope. I had no answers. I was shattered. I had given total commitment to a demanding dream. Now in the face of reality, this dream was inadequate — only half good, a half-truth. Just as a dedicated communist, I had been zealous for my cause, but my cause itself had been imperfect.

The horror confronting me was not only the half-faces, like Picasso's half-masks, reaching out at me across Manila like nightmares. It was a realization that I had been betrayed — that I had betrayed myself and in doing so had betrayed others. We had taught boldly and been taught thoroughly that discipleship was individualistic and 'spiritual': that our responsibility was to teach, to preach and to disciple (i.e. to impart truths about prayer, the Bible, the devotional life and the Holy Spirit and to 'save souls').

But in answer to the cries of these pock-marked poor we'd turned our backs, calling over our shoulder, 'Am I my brother's keeper?'

That question reverberated in the depths of my soul as I hurried, dazed, from appointment to appointment, finding a mother sleeping in the street in her little mobile cart, a man with putrid, festering sores begging for help, another wasted with the yellow colour of a destroyed liver. Where was the social component to my discipleship?

In the answer to that question lay the reworking of an entire lifestyle and belief system. Our training had commended non-involvement in the great social issues of our time. I now had to admit that my years of teaching and preaching a 'spiritual' discipleship had been misguided. Although friends might reject me as having lost my singlemindedness and total commitment, I would have to repent of my error and seek a Jesus-style discipleship. This involved going back to the scriptures to find a discipleship that brought together all of life — social, economic, political, spiritual — under the Lordship of Jesus Christ, a discipleship that dealt with today's injustices.

I had never heard an exposition about the biblical responsibility to transform the social institutions of a city that had made no provision for a pock-marked widow, or for example of how to help a poor squatter landlady oppressing those yet poorer as they rented her squatter home. Discipleship surely meant that disciples had to find Jesus' answers for the exploited factory workers, and how the poor should respond to the money lenders (who demanded their six pesos tomorrow for the five they gave you today). The Bible surely had something to teach about what we should do with such problems of oppression.

Discipleship also had to deal with the slums themselves, as well as with the peasants who cannot cope in an industrial society. It had to deal with the animism and spirit worship that still clutched at the inner Filipino soul, just as for centuries these have had to be exorcised from the Anglo-Saxon soul.

I had given a hundred pesos. But the woman had asked for my life. One evening on a rock in the middle of a park where I used to pray, I reconfirmed my commitment to give my life to bringing what has come to be known as 'holistic discipleship' to the masses of Asia's cities.

Culturally-determined discipleship
The first step amongst Filipino church leaders in moving from 'spiritual' to a holistic discipleship has been the process of adapting Western models of discipleship.

Evangelism can often be successful in a foreign culture, with little effort extended in understanding the cultural values. The missionary, however, who wishes to make disciples must go deep into the soul of the people.

Why? Because a disciple of Christ is one who follows the disciplines of Christ. Many think of these as the scheduling of set times of prayer, Bible reading and so on. But Christ gave little teaching on such things (except to avoid parading them). His are the disciplines of the inner man, the disciplines of the Beatitudes and the Sermon on the Mount — qualities such as humility, meekness and peacemaking. These involve the transformation of the inner soul of a person. That inner soul is deeply moulded by one's culture, a culture that may include values close to those of Christ, while others will be directly opposed to him. The perception of which values need transformation, at which stage of Christian development and in which way this can be accomplished requires a deep understanding of any culture. The role of the missionary developing an indigenous movement is to understand these forces, acting as a catalyst to such changes within the movement's leadership. I was most fortunate that Gene Tabor,

Boni Arzadon and other leaders of the *Lakas-Angkan* movement over many years had succeeded in rethinking an American pattern of ministry from within a Filipino cultural framework. Few other groups have been as successful in this process.

Many of us have a low view of disciplemaking, considering it as imparting basic Bible doctrine. Many also rapidly tie down concepts of discipleship into programs and packages. This is an important component of ministry within a specific sub-cultural grouping, but such packages are not transferable to other cultures. The resultant lack of cultural relevance is seen in reproduced Western church structures, Western church buildings, Western worship patterns and Western Bible school training.

Fortunately along with their graciousness, hospitality and charm, Filipinos are one of the world's most adaptive peoples. The gospel continues to be integrated into their culture despite Western inadequacies in mission strategy and theology.

But disciplemaking is the transmission of life to life. It is caught, not taught. It is a fire that breeds fire. It is not a method, a program, nor even the teaching and preaching of the word of God — though all of these are involved. Disciplemaking is God's love being poured out through one life into another, until the second life catches that love. It is faith imparted by one to another. It is an absolute commitment to the word of God, communicated in the midst of ministry pressures as men and women co-labour together.

(a) First steps

This process of culturally appropriate discipleship can be shown in the story of Manuel, one of the middle-class professionals whom I came to know. He was a final year college student. I was invited to a delicious supper of stuffed fish, rice and other dishes served by the longstanding cook of this family. Manuel was an easy person to relate to. After supper we sat down together and discussed question by question a Bible study entitled 'Assurance of Salvation'.

Even in this first study, culture affected the content of the follow-up. Three factors were constantly in my mind as we discussed the passages.

First, Catholicism has used biblical terms, but given them different meanings. The result is that, for many, it takes weeks for the gospel to become clear.

Second, many in poor societies have grown up in broken family relationships. For such it may take months to establish a clear picture of God the Father as just, merciful, dependable and loving.

Third, since the basic culture is rooted in animism, basic follow-up begins by confrontation with a world view of a pantheon of good and evil spirits.

(b) Person-to-person

Follow-up is best accomplished in the context of a deep personal relationship.

In the highly-structured, time-conscious, impersonal culture of the West, this biblical principle of the worth of the individual has been reduced down by many discipling groups to a concept of 'person-to-person'. This involves, amongst other things, a weekly meeting of an hour to an hour-and-a-half for sharing in Bible study and prayer, and reviewing the memorized word. It is an extremely powerful technique in an individualistic Western culture.

But in a traditional, group-oriented, personal, creative, emotive society, with a time consciousness that is cyclic and event-oriented and a keen sense of the occasion, such a methodology is disastrous.

Personal discipling is extremely threatening methodology to someone who has grown up rarely being alone — and usually never alone (unless married) with only one other person. In Asia, personal relationships are expressed by accompanying someone somewhere, in assisting someone to do something or in attending a family function.

The principle of transferring truth in the context of a deep personal relationship is universal, but its specific cultural form is not cross-cultural. The ancient biblical principles of discipleship remain unchanged, but they are expressed in different cultural forms, with an appropriate fit between biblical and contemporary culture.

(c) Group discipling

Since the command to make disciples was given to a group of men and women who were to disciple men and women, I believed that Manuel would come through to discipleship only if we reached his *barkada* around him (a *barkada* is a group of close-knit friends). I prayed for the opportunity to meet them.

The next time I visited Manuel, his drinking mates were sitting around the table with him. He was watching me carefully to see how I would cope, to see if I could relate. Having asked his sister for a cup of tea and joked our way through numerous introductions, the questions began to come.

Half-drunk men are painfully realistic. We talked a lot about that unusual person, Jesus Christ, and about trust.

'I trust no one, not even my closest friend!' declared one of the *barkada*, looking around at his closest friends. He was a Muslim. His father had had three wives, so he had grown up in an atmosphere of distrust. We talked of Jesus and his forgiveness, but the Muslim was too far drunk to consider trusting the man from Galilee.

After a while I took my leave, having made friends for myself but not yet for the Master.

I must have made an impression, for the next week Manuel brought his girlfriend Celia and two other friends to a Bible study in my squatter home. My cooking was not up to such an occasion, so Celia cooked while we discussed how we could know God's forgiveness.

The week after, Henry, one of these friends, was high on drugs during the study. Two days later, he decided to leave his home, so he brought his belongings over with him to my place. We discussed the word of God about obedience to parents and sent him back home.

Celia was not yet Christian, so I took Celia and Manuel out for a meal in the restaurant in the park. We discussed how to get Henry off drugs, then I explained to Celia how she, too, could know she has eternal life. She was really happy about this.

(d) Animism

One time, Manuel shared with me about the problem he was having memorizing scripture. He would sit in his room, but every time he took out his verse pack to memorize, the lights would die. When he put it away, the lights would return.

I began to question further since, some years before, we had been praying for his older sister to be released from demonic attacks.

In such a context, what are the first steps in disciplemaking? Is not basic follow-up to confront the occult powers, to transform the people's world view, showing clearly the difference between the kingdom of God and the kingdoms of this world? It was some months later that we went up and prayed, commanding the spirit to leave.

(e) Catholicism

To free Manuel and his sister, I needed the whole family to renounce any dealings with the spirit world, including putting away their Catholic idols — statues of the Virgin and of the saints.

Many of the leading church-planters in the Philippines have

come to a position of avoiding direct confrontation with Catholicism (Filipinos are a non-confrontational people), preferring to teach new believers about the Bible and Christian discipleship. The believers very quickly cease praying to Mary upon learning the power of prayer. At times idols are publicly burnt, but mostly they are quietly taken down and hidden, destroyed or, if family heirlooms, given to others in the family. In the same way as it takes months, even years, for believers to cease their drinking, gambling and immorality (oscillating between these and prayer and Bible study meetings), so it takes a similar period for believers to assemble together into worship. At this point of clear stability of commitment and life, it appears wise to baptize believers. Earlier baptism is seen by the family only as a sign of conversion to Protestantism, not as a sign of repentance from sin. As such, it severely limits any further evangelism amongst the Catholics.

It is often difficult for a converted priest to continue in the Catholic priesthood if his commitment to the word of God is in direct conflict with his vows to teach certain dogmas. For the common people, however, untaught in the dogmas of the church, there is no ethical issue that would force them immediately to leave the church. Those that place Christ as Lord and follow the teachings of the scripture seem to be able to remain within the Catholic Church for some years and have a dynamic ministry there. Protestants or Catholics who place a commitment to their church and tradition above their commitment to Christ seem not to come into any fulness of the Spirit or of ministry (though they may have experiences of God).

The basic point of confrontation in follow-up, then, is not primarily with the Catholic Church, but with the underlying animism (the worship of spirits) within the Filipino culture, which has sadly contaminated Catholicism.

(f) Evangelism

The next step in discipling Manuel was to train him in evangelism. Jesus trained his men by taking them with him. The thrust of evangelism in the Philippines is family Bible studies. Another friend had begun a Bible study in the home of his aunt in a squatter area. Three of the women had become believers. I took Manuel with us, for these people were from a neighbouring language grouping. I used Tagalog. Then, when I reached a familiar story, Manuel would repeat it in their own dialect. In this way he learned to tell the gospel better than I could.

(g) The kingdom first...

After a person begins to grow in faith, the second area of focus in disciplemaking is a realignment of personal goals and ambitions.

At this phase, in a framework of actively working together, people feel free to open up their deeper personal needs. I had involved Reuben, another young Christian, in my work with Manuel. One night he told me of his desire to make money — lots of it — by various schemes. He was quite intelligent, an electrical engineer, so there was little doubt he could do it. But he was finding a conflict in the area of his personal ambitions. As Jesus said, 'You cannot serve God and money'. Very gently we discussed 'But seek first his Kingdom and his righteousness...' (Matthew 6:33).

(h) Symbolic commitments

Filipino discipleship, unlike that of middle-class Anglo-Saxons, is not a series of consistent commitments logically followed through. Filipinos make commitments. But on a far different basis. Filipino commitments often involve deep emotive and symbolic experiences.

I believe that Filipino discipleship is a two-level process. There are initial steps of growth and commitment but the step of total commitment to serve the Lord is deeply emotive, usually occurring after some backsliding or some dramatic experience such as the death of a brother, a ministry trip to a distant island and so on. From this point on the disciple of Christ will make unusual sacrifices in following his Master.

(l) Cultural leadership patterns

In developing the leadership team for Bible studies amongst Manila's professionals, there were numerous other cultural values I needed to learn. Amongst them were the role of women, consensus decision-making and group centredness.

Filipino women are held in higher respect than their counterparts in other cultures. In the Philippines eighty per cent of businesses are run by women. Men are the head, the ultimate authority, but the real decision-making work is done by women. Women usually handle family finances. (An interesting side-effect is that Singer sewing machines are almost always paid for in the Philippines!)

I tried to develop key men for the management of the work. That was a mistake, a trespassing on the woman's role. The men's role was to teach and preach — to be the figureheads. The women were to organize and determine where, when and how.

A second change needed in my leadership style was on formulating the process of decision-making. The leadership team would sit and discuss for hours. The leader should sit and listen, gently feeling out the consensus of the group. If a consensus is not reached in a meeting, no decision can be made. Further discussion may create that critical harmony necessary for decision. Harmony — with others, with God and with nature — are crucial components in most Asian cultures, in contrast to our own culture, where achievement is the ultimate and often only point of evaluation.

Hours of small talk, joking and engaging in apparently time-wasting conversation are critical factors in the Filipino mind for creating the right atmosphere of freedom, harmony and unity.

Planning, too, is developed on a different model. Filipinos, it seems, easily perceive the *ultimate* goal, the glorious vision of a brilliant future. Such is the romance of the Filipino heart. The implications for the present are deduced from this, the group collectively deeply committed to its realization. *Intermediate* goals may be verbalized, but the concrete steps required for their fulfilment are not spelt out in case they restrict the creativity that is the driving force behind Filipino achievements. This is quite a contrast to the highly structured planning models of the West, with their emphasis on pre-planning at every step.

Ministry growth

Because of the deep commitments of the core people amongst these professionals, rather than my inadequate leadership, the group grew rapidly from eighteen to seventy. Where we thought in terms of reaching whole social groups — whole offices, whole families or *barkadas* the ministry increased.

We established monthly fellowships for all the people in Manila, worked towards a college group, a Makati group (the business centre of Manila), a couples' group and a social workers' fellowship. Requests for help kept coming from pastors, students and professionals.

A pastor came by and we spent three hours sitting in the park, discussing the philosophy of disciplemaking. What was the relationship of discipling and the development of gifts? The answer to this would not be revealed to me until two years later in the New Zealand revival.

Another was excited about the idea of teaching his church how to have family devotions. It was the first time he'd ever thought to have prayer times with his elders. There was a real breakthrough. Family devotions began to become a regular part of church life.

What does a missionary working amongst Manila's middle-class do? I usually preached two or three times weekly and enjoyed double-teaming with my leader who had responsibility for the development of the whole movement. It is the role I enjoy most in the ministry — supporting another, complementing, encouraging. It requires a dexterity far more demanding than being the kingpin and a greater depth of emotional maturity, so was a challenging exercise. It was encouraging to see the result of a similar supportive relationship from my earlier years in Manila. (There were now several disciplemakers in the first church we had been involved in planting.)

The ministry involved extensive counselling. I had a former student come and stay in my home. He, like most without a local church base, went back to his old lifestyle — in this case, homosexuality.

I also met weekly with ten to twenty people and was involved in extensive counselling and training. Much of my time had been spent travelling for weekends to minister with others on the staff to the outlying agricultural universities. We put together manuals on the basics of Christian growth and follow-up for these three day trips. The men who made up the teams during these trips are now leaders of these ministries.

The climas of my work with the professionals and in the wider ministry of the *Lakas-Angkan* movement came with the opportunity to lead a training program for 194 leaders from the core groups of each of the thirteen agricultural university ministries. One day we split program trainees into groups of fifteen and sent them out to the barrios to 'preach the gospel to the poor'. Each group developed a drama, some special musical items and testimonies, while one of the men preached. Over 100 came to Christ. One of the men was so excited after this experience of preaching to the poor that the next month he gathered together a team to preach in the Bicol area of Tatalon.

Economic repentance
My New Zealand comrades had enough exposure to missions theory to appreciate these cultural deviations from the norm, but what was most disconcerting for them — and threatening — was the economic implications of this kind of discipleship.

I had already been meeting some small economic and social

needs. Four rabbits happily played outside the window of my room. I was experimenting to see if these might be a way of supplementing my regular intake of meat. I would go jogging each morning, collecting grass and ipil-ipil leaves for them on the way. Eventually I concluded that rabbits were too complex a husbandry project for most poor families.

I invested some money in a goat for Ka Emilio in Lipa City. He eventually sold it when he found he was too old to keep taking it out to find grass — especially in the wet season.

For years my co-labourers in the *Lakas-Angkan* movement had had a deep commitment to meeting socio-economic needs. This had been demonstrated symbolically in a pig farm. The six-week-old piglets were given to poor families, who raised them to seven months on food scraps and then sold them, making a small sum to supplement their income. This farm was also a training centre to help educated Filipinos learn to work with their hands. It was at the same time a centre for economic projects. We spent some time and effort to recruit money from Tear Fund for an air lift-pump developed by a Canadian friend for the farm. He believed it would lower the price of the average farmer's pump to one tenth. It was a demonstration of our commitment to small scale, appropriate technology — technical projects at the technical and economic levels of the people.

After writing a few thoughts home to New Zealand on these economic projects, I received some letters asking if perhaps I had moved from my commitment to disciplemaking as the thrust of mission. I sought to answer these comments honestly, communicating my growing understanding. They served, as letters normally do, to confuse. I wrote:

I have begun to realize how much our Western culture has moulded my view of the scriptures, how in most areas of our lives we compartmentalize: the social is not the spiritual is not the economic. We have a great divide in our thinking which can be illustrated thus:

$$\frac{\text{Spiritual issues} \ = \ \text{religion}}{\substack{\text{Social-economic-} \\ \text{political issues} \ = \ \text{life}}}$$

But the scriptures are not Western; they are Eastern. They see life as a whole; they are holistic.

Discipleship involves the spiritual, i.e. our relationship to God. However, even in the great commission, Jesus includes social and economic repentance along with proclamation to preach. He tells us not only to 'go, make disciples...' but to 'teach them to *observe* all' that he had commanded (Matthew 20:19). Observance involves action. The action is evidenced socially, economically, even politically:

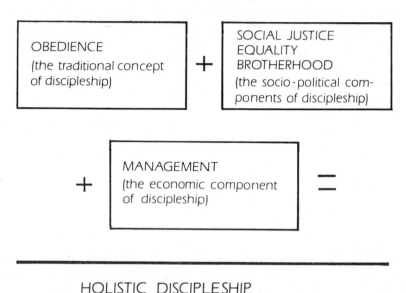

OBEDIENCE (the traditional concept of discipleship)	+	SOCIAL JUSTICE EQUALITY BROTHERHOOD (the socio-political components of discipleship)

+ MANAGEMENT (the economic component of discipleship) =

HOLISTIC DISCIPLESHIP
(the biblical concept of discipleship)

One evening during this time I was speaking to a fellowship, talking of repentance. I mentioned John the Baptist's demand: 'He who has two coats, let him share with him who has none, and he who has food let him do likewise' (Luke 3:11).

As I spoke, I was struck by the fact that I had never before spoken of economic repentance when I had been preaching the gospel. The repentance I had spoken of had been purely in spiritual terms. From this time on my preaching would define repentance economically, spiritually, socially and, where necessary, politically. It transformed my evangelism.

A development of the bridge diagram we had often used to portray the gospel now looked like this:

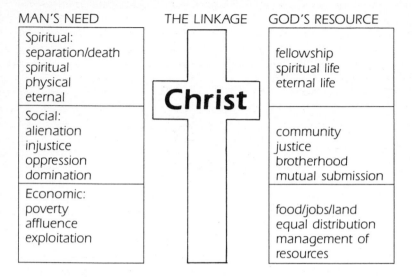

MAN'S NEED	THE LINKAGE	GOD'S RESOURCE
Spiritual: separation/death spiritual physical eternal	**Christ**	fellowship spiritual life eternal life
Social: alienation injustice oppression domination		community justice brotherhood mutual submission
Economic: poverty affluence exploitation		food/jobs/land equal distribution management of resources

Jesus might be the answer, but as Christians we had not been asking the right questions. Western notions of the gospel and discipleship were irrelevant in the Third World except to the upper- and middle-class, whose problems related primarily to psychological, and emotional needs.

Mission and the gospel
What, then, are our social, economic and political responsibilities of disciples of Christ?

The following responsibilities are commonly thought of as 'disciplemaking':

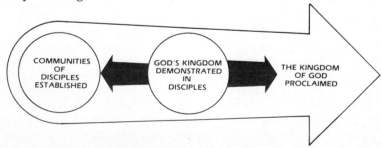

COMMUNITIES OF DISCIPLES ESTABLISHED — GOD'S KINGDOM DEMONSTRATED IN DISCIPLES — THE KINGDOM OF GOD PROCLAIMED

These are primary to all we do, but the scriptures *add* the following principles we are to use to influence the world — as salt keeps meat from rotting and light expels darkness.

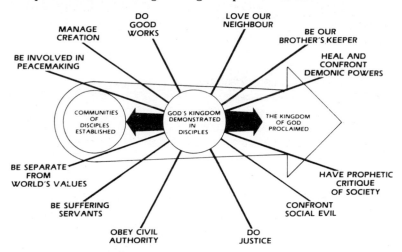

To these general principles, we may add specific commands regarding social, economic and political action.

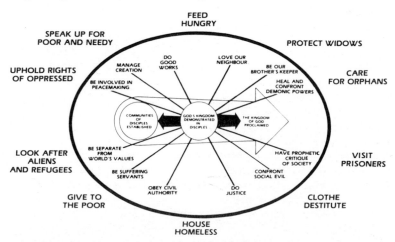

All of the above are part of our mission, as we await the return of our Lord.

Our mission as Christians is primarily to proclaim the truth about God, but we are also to live in the world. Expressing God's life in us involves all of these other factors. We are to be 'our brother's keeper'; we are 'to manage creation'; we are to 'do justice'. This is the context in which God's kingdom is proclaimed.

Free at last

Thus, along with Filipino leaders, our thinking had moved from a Western 'spiritual' concept of discipleship first to a culturally adapted one, then to a holistic discipleship. But there was one more step in my search before God could illuminate a theology and strategy for ministry to the urban poor.

Discipleship had been the theme of my life as it is a dominant theme in the scriptures, but I had become uneasy about making it the centre of my theology. For years I had rejected the dispensational view which divided biblical history into a series of dispensations, in such a way that (though this is never stated) God changes tactics and character in each dispensation. Thus the Old Testament is relegated to irrelevancy by stating its dispensation. Similarly much of Jesus' teaching becomes obsolete. What is left as important is the 'spiritual' teaching of the apostle Paul. Even the apostolic dispensation has finished, and with it miracles, signs and prophetic gifts.

The search culminated one day with explosive illumination -like walking into a floodlit room.

I was sitting in a class studying the theological perspectives of community development.[1] As Dr William Dyrness mapped out God's interventions (a community development term) in history (a theological starting point), God intervened! Suddenly, I saw the universal biblical theme around which all of life as well as ministry to the poor could be integrated. It was the greatness, the fullness, the unity of the Kingdom of God in the scriptures and the immutable, unchanging nature of God himself.

I studied how the economic principles of the Kingdom were first expressed in the life of Israel, in the life of the church. I saw that God's economics, though expressed in different contexts, do not change from age to age, but are universal! Similarly with the politics of God. His truth was unchanging.[2]

In a flash, the Spirit of God showed me the basis for a theology for developing movements amongst squatters. My excitement knew no limits. I devoured article after article, verse after verse, working eighteen hours a day on the task. My years of searching and questioning had, at last, found a focal point. I now needed time to work back from this focal point and develop a total theology for reaching Asia's squatters.

Eric Hoffer points out that popular movements begin with people of words — the *intelligentsia* who capture the feeling, the mood of the times, and bring it to the notice of the people.[3]

I hesitate to call myself an intellectual, but it was such a time in Manila — a time to forge the foundations for a ministry to the squatters from amongst the intellectuals. I sensed that my role, as a foreigner, was to identify the season we were in, recognise God's purpose for the national church and serve it with all my energy. Within a few days God had enabled the writing of a forty-page article entitled 'Christian Perspective on Development Philosophies'. It sought to integrate various biblical material on the kingdom of God, on the poor, on economics and the realities of present Filipino social conditions.

To some, such academic study may seem meaningless. But thought must precede action. Having broken the bonds of a tightly defined theological system, I needed to establish a new basis for mission. Others could follow — and develop new approaches — if the biblical basis was clear.

Harmless as doves

These were also issues of life and death in a highly dangerous political situation where each month government agents reported on my movements.

'When you first came, I thought you were a Marxist worker', said one of the community leaders to me two years later as we were discussing economic projects. She was quite suspicious because the Marxists had entered Tatalon before. They even had given scholarships to people and worked with the Catholic priests.

I had just explained to another friend in her presence how, as Christians, we wanted to put the control of production and exporting into the hands of the poor — to avoid letting the rich gain control of the economic projects, and to develop cottage industries. Unlike the Marxists, we did not intend to use our economic projects to buy people for Christianity. What we wanted was to assist those who *already* had spiritual life to become stable economically, so they could be relieved from peer-group pressures and from personally destructive behaviour like gambling, drunkenness, adultery and drug addiction.

As a regular report was being made on my activities in the slums, it was essential that I be able to define my position. The word, I knew, would be passed on to the appropriate authorities. Discipleship is 'always being ready to give a reason for the hope that is in you'!

As an extra bonus, academic mastery of issues relating to politics, economics and the poor also gave entrance to social workers, community workers, religious leaders and academics in the upper class. From these, I believe, will come many key labourers amongst the poor.

I sat one afternoon discussing the causes of poverty with a professor friend. After ten years of research, she had come to realize that the environmental factors are only secondary causes of slum poverty. We discussed how the evil that comes out of the heart — such as oppression, exploitation, violence and laziness (whether bureaucratic or working class) — is itself a significant factor in causing poverty. The immorality of the poor themselves also sires poverty. We discussed how the gospel is good news to the poor since it sets them free, causing the poor to be uplifted and the rich to repent of their oppression.

Twelve theologians from across Asia spent a year studying issues of poverty. Other Filipino evangelical Christians were voicing their theologies of community development. It was important to keep in touch with these mainstreams of prophetic witness in the church. Proverbs tells us 'in the abundance of counsellors is wisdom'. The work amongst the poor grew from such counsellors at the coalface of Filipino theology.

One of these was Pastor Johnny, the leader of a church we had been involved in establishing some years earlier. Early one morning we met in the park as the dawn glowed from pink to blue. We discussed how Jesus' ethical teaching on right relationships leads into Paul's theology of economic and social responsibility. Then we talked through a strategy for work amongst the poor.

There were a number of social workers involved in Bible studies. We sought to draw them together to discuss the biblical basis of social work. They had been taught the empty shell of a deaconess' work by humanist professors, but had not yet been able to fully integrate their work and their faith. Some were trapped into social work without a biblical base. Discipleship had affected their personal lives in areas of prayer and Bible study; they wanted it to become the heart of their work. These social workers had already begun to bring significant biblical reforms into government and aid agencies.

Over several weeks during the same period, six other graduates met together for a series of studies on the economic implications of discipleship. We discussed issues such as creating work, earning money, caring for the environment, being effective managers of finance, and discovering the responsibilities of the rich to the poor.

These times resulted in a booklet entitled 'Finances and the Kingdom of God' and a number of one-day seminars.

Developing these ideas like this had one tangible benefit: the major components of the theology behind our squatter movement were now on paper. The next phase of ministry was now to clearly map out a strategy for the work.

Footnotes on Chapter 5

1. Some introductory papers to a theology of community development are: Bruce Nicholls, 'Theology for the People', *Evangelical Review of Theology*, October 1978, pp 236-253;
   Evangelicals and Development Towards a Theology of Social Change, ed. Ronald Sider, Paternoster Press, 1981;
   'Christian Forum, Issue on Development', Vol. IV, 1980-81, Journal of Philippine Missionary Institute, Registrar, PMI, Silang, Cavite, Philippines.
2. Perhaps the best portrayal of the biblical theology of the kingdom of God is George Eldon Ladd, *The Gospel of the Kingdom*, Eerdmans, 1959
3. Eric Hoffer, *The True Believer*, Harper and Row, 1966

6

To Have or Not to Have?

ECONOMICALLY JUST LIFESTYLES

DISCIPLEMAKING IS A COMMITMENT of one life to another through thick and thin. Knowing I was not called to these professionals, I could not give my heart to them. I could not be a true pastor; disciplemaking could not really occur. All I could do was to set a framework, a structure, and handle the problems as they occurred.

The office Bible studies continued to multiply; the university groups began to come together; a graduate group began at the University of the Philippines; several pastors were asking for help. The ministry grew from seventy to a hundred professionals and college students. And God was giving freedom in preaching after five years of the hard discipline of developing the skills of telling stories and of crafting sermons.

But the call of the poor still beat relentlessly in my mind. An inner compulsion continued within: I must take the gospel to the poor. All my creative energy must be directed towards the poor, the needy and the broken. But the cost in doing so would be my personal relationships with my middle-class co-labourers as I sought to involve them with me.

How does one involve the middle-class and rich in the needs of the poor? What lifestyle is appropriate for them to live? What models do we have from the past?

Substance and simplicity

Job and Abraham are interesting examples of rich men with a deep commitment to the poor. Both were patriarchs, men of great social standing and influence, living at a time when society was built around a clan structure.

Abraham was a man committed to simplicity of lifestyle. Though he had great wealth, he employed it wisely to support his hundreds of dependants (a model for factory owners!). Though he knew how to build cities, having grown up in Ur of the Chaldees, he chose to live simply in a tent. As Hebrews tells us: 'By faith, he sojourned in the land of promise, as in a foreign land, living in tents with Isaac and Jacob, heirs with him of the same promise. For he looked forward to the city which has foundations whose builder and maker is God' (11:9-10).

Such men can be used to minister to the poor. Abraham established a pattern which is consistent throughout the scriptures: 'The blessing of the Lord makes rich and he adds no sorrow with it' (Proverbs 10:22). Yet those who have wealth are not to live luxuriously but simply — 'to be rich in good deeds, liberal and generous. . . for the love of money is the root of all evil' (1 Timothy 6:6-8, 10 and 18).

In the scriptures, greed (or covetousness) and excessive luxury are just as bad sins as immorality or adultery (Ephesians 5:3-5). Indeed we are not even to have lunch with a brother who is greedy (1 Corinthians 5:11).

For any person who would live out a gospel of justice and grace, to live luxuriously is to be a party to injustice. Piety and luxury cannot coexist! Living luxuriously in the midst of poverty is a denial of justice:

> if anyone has this world's goods and sees his brother in need, yet closes his heart against him, how does God's love abide in him? (1 John 3:17).

To be obedient to this command surely means that nobody should have excessively more than others. The poor should be uplifted, the rich brought low and equality should result. (Though clearly we don't keep giving till we too become destitute for then we only add ourselves to the problem.)

And clearly there is a need for some men to have capital, as Abraham had capital. But to use it to benefit the workers, as he used it to benefit his people.

Job, the greatest of all the patriarchs of the East, also had great capital. He too used it to benefit his people. In his justifications, Job describes how to be a godly rich man:

I delivered the poor (**ani**) who cried,
and the fatherless who had none to help him.
I caused the widow's heart to sing for joy,
I put on righteousness, and it clothed me
my justice was like a robe and turban.
I was eyes to the blind
and feet to the lame;
I was a father to the poor (**ebyon**),
and I searched out the cause of him
whom I did not know.
I broke the fangs of the unrighteous,
and made him drop his prey from his teeth (Job 29:12-17).

In summary, rich people are to live simply and use their capital to benefit the poor. This is justice. For a Western missionary or a Christian businessman to live otherwise is a great evil.

The poor have an intuitive knowledge of such issues. They know it is unjust that I am a rich man and they are poor. Of course everyone, rich and poor, know that riches are a gift from God and that sin is a cause of poverty. But the poor man of understanding knows more than a rich man who is wise in his own eyes. He knows it is often the sins of oppression, exploitation and injustice committed in the name of 'fair profit' that have made him poor.

So it is just for him to *expect* assistance from the rich! The rich man's wealth, the white man's money, has to a large extent been made on the backs of the peasants, through hundreds of years of exploitation of the Third World. We owe the poor a debt! We are expected to give! This is justice!

This logic is unshakeably rational. It is also very painful to me, a rich Westerner.

But justice is not to live in equal *destitution* with the destitute. Justice for Jesus was to live humbly, simply, without excess and share whatever he had with those around — to share with the destitute. Justice was to not have more than that required by our daily needs — 'Give us this day our daily bread' — and yet, at the same time, it was to enjoy all the good things God has made.

In seeking a just society, to live as poor amongst the poor, we cannot live a life of destitution — the destitute poor have no respect for this themselves. They themselves are moving upwards, at least to the level of sufficiency for their own needs.

This is personal justice:

There is great gain in godliness with contentment; for we brought nothing into the world, and we cannot take anything out of the world; but if we have food and clothing, with these we shall be content (1 Timothy 6:6-8).

There have been other rich men like St Francis of Assissi, who have needed for the salvation of their own souls to follow another command given by Jesus to the rich young ruler:

If you would be perfect, go, sell what you possess and give to the poor, and you will have treasure in heaven; and come, follow me (Matthew 19:21).

My observation is that most converted rich are encouraged to do as Abraham and Job — to remain rich, but use their wealth wisely; to turn their income into capital which can create work for the poor; to live simply yet not be destitute. Unfortunately, few of us can hang on to our wealth and on to Jesus at the same time, despite the continual output of testimonies by the wealthy and the perversion of 'prosperity theology'. This theology teaches a 'be saved and get rich' Christianity by building on the teaching of the Pentateuch, Job and Proverbs about the righteous rich, but ignoring the Psalms, prophets and teaching of Jesus about the godly poor. This approach works against genuine spirituality. In the house church movement amongst the rich of Djakarta, believers sagely use the phrase 'Repent of your sins, then repent of your wealth'!

In the Manila context, wealth is a complex issue. To live amongst the squatters and then be found eating in some rich restaurant with some 'rich' Western missionaries destroys one's identification with the poor. We have almost to choose one lifestyle or the other. The choice of a ministry to the poor, it seems, precludes a ministry to the middle-class!

Commitment without identification

But is there a reasonable lifestyle for middle-class Filipinos who desire to minister to the poor?

Here we may cite Lazarus, Mary and Martha as examples of the middle-class of Israel. They had a large home. They kept it and used it for the Lord and his disciples as a retreat centre.

People often ask 'Were you called to minister to the poor?' The response can only be: 'We are all called to minister to the poor.

Such a ministry is the logical obedience of any disciple imitating the attitudes, character and teaching of Jesus. He commands everyone to renounce all (Luke 14:33), to give to the poor and live simply. However, not all are called to a life of *identification* with the poor by living amongst them!' On the other hand, one would need a very special call to minister primarily to the rich or middle-class, for the focus of Christian ministry is 'good news to the poor!'

I have not discerned God calling many of my middle-class friends to lives of identification with the poor. There were some who heard and refused his call, but in general the Lord was calling them to a ministry amongst their middle-class peers. To expect them to choose identification with the poor was to expect them to become apostles and missionaries across a great social, economic and cultural barrier.

For just as the missionary community was trapped by structures, expectations and affluence into middle- and upper-class ministries so the average middle-class Filipino is driven by materialism and the intense demands of upward mobility (through education and post-graduate degrees). Many of the *nouveau riche* have come from genuine poverty. They still consider themselves poor, but are compelled by family responsibilities to keep moving up to take their family out of poverty. The poor constitute a danger to this class. Any relationship to poor people outside of their own clan would drain hard-won finances.

To expect people from this class to jump the class barrier and live amongst the poor was expecting more than I myself had sacrificed. Never having experienced *involuntary* poverty it was much easier for me, as a 'rich Westerner' and a member of the 'upper class' to choose *voluntary* poverty. I still had resources, security and friends. But for a person growing up, waging personal and family warfare with maiden poverty, there is no romance in returning to a life of frugality.

The Catholic Church has followed this path. It has orders which choose poverty. But these same orders have plenty of material assets, plenty of financial security. From their position of security, they do not call men and women to total insecurity.

Nevertheless like Lazarus, Mary and Martha, the middle-class can have a significant commitment to the poor. Some fifteen of these middle-class co-labourers have spent extensive time assisting in Tatalon, some making attempts to help economically, some with a Bible study group with a poor family. Others would come and stay overnight, others for two or three weeks, to provide some degree of companionship.

Early on, a whole team made an evangelistic foray into the community. A number were already implementing biblical reforms in their office work because of their commitment to justice. Most gave at times to needy believers. As these men and women rise in government, in business and in the academic world, it is certain they will propagate many reforms and principles as the result of the deep commitments formed during these early years of holistic discipleship. Already in the provincial ministries many poor are being reached through student outreach. Many projects have been proposed, many plans made of ways to help the poor. These are some of the good things God desires of the middle-class.

To call such people to live amongst the poor was difficult. The best I could do was to set the pace, trusting God to inspire some others.

And I could speak of Jesus who tells us:

> As thou didst send me into the world,
> so I have sent them into the world (John 17:18).

The Carpenter's justice

He had been born as a little babe in a dairy shed; he grew up as a refugee child. His parents were so poor they could not afford a sheep at his dedication and so had to offer two turtle doves. Tradition tells us that as a teenager he worked to support his mother and family. He chose to be a scribe, men renowned for their poverty, rather than a rich high priest. He had no place to lay his head. He had calloused hands, wore wooden sandals and died a poor man's death.

He was Jesus, the just one! Nobody could fault him for economic injustice in his standard of living. Justice demanded equality between sent one and people. Justice demanded identification or, as the Marxists term it, 'solidarity' with the poor. He lived at the level of the people, identifying himself with them in voluntary simplicity.

Yet, he lived without destitution! He was not a beggar; he was not unemployed. He provided for his twelve followers through the ministry of some women (Luke 8:4). He had sufficient.

Yet Jesus, the just one, asked more from his middle-class companions than acceptance of the status quo. He demanded renunciation of possessions:

> So therefore, whoever of you does not renounce all that he has cannot be my disciple (Luke 14:33).

He told his team:

> Fear not, little flock . . . Sell your possessions, and give alms; provide yourself with purses that do not grow old, with a treasure in the heavens that does not fail . . . (Luke 12:32-33).

Jesus here used the word 'forsake' or 'renounce'. It is an action word; it is not just an attitude.

Many of us would like it to focus purely on attitude: 'Whoever has many possessions, but uses them wisely will be my disciple'. But Jesus was very blunt. It is junk or Jesus. Just junk *or* just Jesus — not junk *and* Jesus. Forsake first as an attitude, but let the attitude result in action.

'You cannot serve God and affluence,' says Jesus elsewhere (Matthew 6:24). Not 'may not', but *cannot*! There is no choice.

But what does Jesus mean by renouncing *all*? He himself grew up in a good home, possessed carpenter's tools, probably played with toys as a child and had a common purse (bank account) with the disciples. He wore clothes. He had breakfast each morning. He tells us in Matthew 6 that the Father will provide our food and clothing!

'Food and clothing' is a phrase for our basic necessities. It may include shelter, work tools, books, children's toys, decorations and provision for celebration. In most situations today this involves buying a home — just as the Levites were to own no possessions in Israel, but they were to have their own home and enough garden to provide for themselves. But the same phrase excludes a life of ease, luxury and wealth. It is not a call to destitute poverty, but it *is* a call to simplicity. Just as involuntary and destitute poverty has no intrinsic virtue, so wealth is often destructive of spirituality.

The attitudes involved are important. At issue is whether we will eliminate external, glittering possessions and follow him, developing an internal concentration on him — unfettered and unhindered by excess material baggage.

One way to apply this, a symbolic start, is to sit down with our families and go through each of our possessions and use of finance with the purpose of getting rid of all excess — whatever detracts in time, money and energy from Christ.

Celebration!

But Jesus was no ascetic. He came eating, drinking and enjoying life, and was much criticised by the Bible-believers of his day for his lack of frugality.

Job, too, enjoyed feasting and drinking; the Old Testament is replete with commands for festivals and celebrations. We need to live out a 'celebrating lifestyle of renunciation'.

Ironically, the conflict between the biblical concepts of celebration and renunciation was resolved in my mind one day as I was sitting relaxing with some middle-class friends eating ice-cream! The Lord brought to mind the passage immediately preceding his call to renunciation:

> When you give a dinner or a banquet, do not invite your. . .
> rich neighbours. . . But when you give a feast, invite the poor,
> the maimed, the lame, the blind, and you will be blessed,
> because they cannot repay you (Luke 14:12-14).

We are to enjoy life, but *with* and *for* the poor and needy. We are to die to our economic selves, but we are to live glorious economic resurrection lives for others.

My ministry to middle-class Filipinos could be summed up by the following five slogans:

Earn much
Consume little
Hoard nothing
Give generously
Celebrate life.

The offence of identification

If I could not freely call the middle-class to identification with the poor, I could set a pattern of identification. It appeared the most effective way to call the rich to ministry amongst the poor was by personally offering them the one thing they did not have: the joy of the Lord in the midst of poverty. But I concluded that it would be faster and wiser to call others who had grown up through involuntary poverty — labouring men who could provide for themselves, but were unafraid of the rough and tough of voluntary poverty. So the first step in defining any strategy was to return to living amongst the squatters.

But this in itself is a dilemma. For to live *amongst* the poor is seen as a judgement on middle-class models of ministry *to* the poor. Identification itself is offensive. I have never resolved this problem except by love, communication and obedience. My responsibility to my friends and leaders is to be obedient to the call of God.

This came home to me one time when a women's leader came to me in distress. We were involved in an exorcism and so she had been searching her life to see if there was any sin. She confronted me:

'Viv, I want to apologise for something. I've been deeply offended that you should be living here!'

Over the years I've realised what a rebuke identification is. In some senses it is saying 'Why don't you look after your own poor?' But to choose identification is not primarily an action to shame other Christians. It is obedience to the compulsion of compassion.

There were other friends who disagreed with my desire to identify. One time I visited a highly trained and experienced social worker amongst the squatters. For two hours we talked and discussed, across a coffee table in the shady porch of her house, our mutual dream of reaching the poor. Inwardly, she was laughing at this foolish foreigner who would attempt to live amongst the squatters, obviously without understanding of the risks and pressures involved.

I smiled back. 'Yes, it is impossible. The possible anyone can do. But the impossible? Ah, that's different. That's what God would want to do and I want to be in on it. It will take time. It is impossible now, but time will make it possible.'

7
Point of Attack
DISCERNING A MINISTRY STRATEGY

WE KNEW OF NO MISSIONARIES who had chosen to work amongst the squatters and plant churches. So I began searching amongst the aid agencies for patterns or models of ministry. I considered also people of God in history who had walked the path of poverty.

I talked with one friend, a social work researcher who had compared the work of World Vision and the Salvation Army in her Master's thesis.

We enthused over General Booth's original scheme for reaching London in the 1890s and its applicability to Manila in the 1980s.[1] We laughed at the difference between Booth and myself. He was tough. He came from amongst the poor. He was an evangelist. I find it hard to live amongst the poor, let alone to minister effectively to them. I am not tough.

As a result of this discussion, I visited the leader of the Salvation Army Social Services. He was a sandy-haired Englishmen dressed in the century-ancient Salvation Army uniform. He was flanked by beautiful, smiling Filipino faces, all in similar English-style uniforms. Such is the amazing Filipino adaptability and capacity to integrate other cultures!

Apart from certain cultural anachronisms, I was deeply impressed by their work in the slums. It was small but effective, combining vocational training with Christian ministry. A year later I had an hour with this man of God when a bus I was travelling on broke down. I was off-loaded on to the succeeding bus and, sighting a familiar white face, squeezed into a neighbouring seat. We were both making a nine-hour journey.

I learned a great deal from him about saving people's souls and transforming their environment.

Kagawa of Japan

But my biggest encouragement was the life of another who had suffered no encouragement at first: Kagawa of Japan. It is his life that gave me a realistic model of how to integrate evangelism with the fight against poverty. Over the years have been added to the hall of fame the lives of Calvin, Finney, Booth, Wesley, Assissi, Xavier, Mother Teresa, Dom Helder Camara and many others committed to the poor.

There are marked differences in the lives of these people. Yet all understood the centrality of preaching. And all understood the necessity of focussing on the poor as a priority.

Kagawa, Assissi and Xavier lived as poor men amongst the poor. Booth, Wesley and Calvin chose simple lifestyles. All moved from lives as pure evangelists to become evangelist social reformers: fighters against sin and fighters against poverty and social injustice at every level of society.

Kagawa began with a commitment to identification, choosing to live in the slums of Shinkawa. But he soon realised that a 'spiritual' approach of preaching and teaching alone was insufficient. However, those early years were full of the essential experiences of identification. It was through the positive response to his work in these years that the next phase of his work was founded.

From evangelist he moved to being evangelist social worker, starting a small dispensary and distributing food to beggars. But during a time of study in the United States he realized that he must work at the level of social reform if he was to rescue these slum people.

TB was rife where people were undernourished and their hours of work long. The work hours had to be shortened by legislation.

Prostitution was a consequence of poverty. That poverty must be dealt with if he would save many of these young believers from returning to this lifestyle. Drink was an escape mechanism. Labour demanded legislation if it was not to be exploitive. At this point, Kagawa realised he had been so busy working amongst the slum people that he had not thought about dealing with the problem of the slums themselves.

On his return to Shinkawa he soon saw that, though much had been done, many of the things for which he had laboured so hard had been lost. The mission was continuing, but without his personal active interference on the side of righteousness the young people had failed to withstand the forces of evil. Three of the girls

A section of Tatalon: 14,500 people per square mile

Squatter homes: erected from any available plywood and galvanized iron

Viv Grigg's home: up the stairs, first on the left

Outside the house: venue for the first Bible studies

Aling Nena (right), Eleanor her daughter and Metzai her neice

Boy, Tess and family. Boy is a carpenter, inventor and leader of the young believers. Tess is daughter of the <u>barrio</u> councillor, one of twenty-five graduates and developer of the rag-making and other economic projects.

Pastor Jun, Milleth and Jedidiah

Pastor Jun and household: wife, son, mother, sister and brother

had been sold as prostitutes and forty of the boys were in prison for theft and other crimes. These things deepened his convictions that the problem of poverty itself would have to be tackled.

'We must get rid of poverty... force the Government to acknowledge the workers' rights to form unions... sweep away the slums,' he preached.

There was embarrassment, anger and hostility. Talk about political action or economic schemes and the reply was always the same: 'It isn't the job of the church.'

Kagawa saw that his future was bound up with three demands:

(a) He must show that Christianity was not a pietistic way of life, remote from the joyful yet dirty business of daily living. He could only demonstrate this by continuing to live in the limiting, sordid environment of Shinkawa.

(b) But alongside his practical compassion, he must go out in the name of Christ and try to find some solution to the labour problem of Japan.

(c) In doing so, he would alienate many of his fellow Christians, as well as expose himself to Government wrath.

From this point he became rapidly involved in the establishing of trade unions — this at a time when they were yet illegal and strikes were still illegal. The power of his leadership was seen in his ability to control strikes with his preaching as much as his readiness to speak in favour of them. His preaching of non-violence enabled the movement to remain out of the hands of the communists at critical points. It was this that finally permitted peaceful negotiations for the existence of trade unions in Japan.

But Kagawa, in speaking to labourers, left no doubt of his own position: 'Unions are necessary — but labour problems can only be solved by a change in the heart of the labourer himself.' Kagawa went on to deal with the cause of urban poverty — rural poverty — and many other major social and political projects. But never did he lose his primary cutting-edge as a preacher of the cross of Christ, eventually standing before the Emperor of Japan to preach the gospel.

Kagawa was an evangelist cum reformer. Assissi, the great 13th century evangelist to the poor and disciplemaker of the rich, was also a wandering evangelist. He, too, was a social reformer, whose preaching led to economic repentance. At one time in his own strife-torn city of Assissi he acted as arbiter between the two factions that rent its peace: the rich, the *majores*, who were in conflict with the poor, the *minores*.

The document drawn up between them compelled the rich to consult the poor in making agreements with other cities. The lords, in consideration of a small, periodical payment were to renounce all the feudal rights; the inhabitants of the villages surrounding Assissi were to be put on a par with those of the city. Foreigners were protected, the assessment of taxes was fixed and the exiled poor were allowed to return.[2]

Save souls... save bodies... save society

'Do we save men's souls or save their environment?' How often have I heard this non-question. The theologians put it in more abstruse terms: 'Do we work for the transformation of the individual or the transformation of the structures of society?'

The questions themselves are in error, resulting from the Greek dichotomy of mankind into spirit and body. The Hebrew concept, Jesus' concept of life, knew no such dichotomy.

As if Kagawa had a choice! He began changing individuals. He soon recognized he must change the individual *and* the environment that holds him in his bondage.

As if I have a choice between saving souls and saving bodies, between the spiritual and political when, beside by friend's house, is a vacant lot covered with rat-infested garbage. The politicians had called a meeting, discussed the need and even had a garbage pit dug, but still the field of garbage grew. So I asked the Christians to bring shovels. For a whole morning we shovelled the putrid rotting food, the rusty cans, the small snakes, cockroaches, ants and poisonous centipedes into the hole and set it alight.

A lady approached from a neighbouring house, 'O praise God!' she said. 'Last night I prayed, "Lord, I am unable alone to shift this rubbish." But day after day the winds blow its disease into my small house. Now, here you are, an answer to prayer.'

I smiled and told her, 'Yes, God is so gracious, isn't he! He wants us not only to be free from the rubbish of the sin in our hearts, so we can be saved; he also wants us to be free from the rubbish in our environment, so we can *live*! He wants us to be rulers over our creation!'

But still the trucks promised by the politicians did not arrive. These squatters had no bribe money; rich businesses did. The garbage filled the field again.

One prayer meeting night with other young squatter believers,

I felt constrained to pray that God would completely get rid of this rubbish beside my friend's house.

The next day, workers came. They pushed the rubbish down the hill into the river ('That wasn't quite what I had in mind, Lord, but thank you anyway'). Then they placed a large sign: 'It is forbidden to throw rubbish here: fine P100. Signed: Barrio Captain'.

We are called to rule creation by work. Salvation enables us to rule also by the authority of the name of Christ in prayer! We are called to save souls. We are called to save the bodies of the chldren who get sick through the disease of a rubbish dump. There is no choice between souls and environment.

The primacy of proclamation

While avoiding the traditional errors of our evangelical heritage in 'spiritualizing' the kingdom of God, a commitment to the scriptures needs, on the other hand, to beware of the traditions of some 'liberal' Protestants at the other end of the pendulum. Their misunderstandings of the nature of truth and hence of the Bible have resulted in defining the aim of mission as socio-economic-political change.

In searching to understand their theology, one day I curled up in a soft chair in the magnificent Manila Peninsula Hotel. (At times I would take a whole day off to get some peace and quiet, and again experience air-conditioning and Western culture. Everybody assumed I was a tourist! God gives us all good things to enjoy!) This day I read right through the Gospel of Mark to see if I could perhaps readapt my thinking on the thrust of mission, to see if there was any way I could accommodate the teaching that the aim of mission is socio-economic-political change.

There was no way. The Gospels are clear. The establishment of the kingdom is accomplished not primarily by political change, economic change or social change. It is accomplished by people preaching the good news that the kingdom of God has come, and people repenting of their sin against God, of their economic exploitation and their social hatreds, and submitting themselves to the teaching of the King. With this proclamation are to be demonstrations of spiritual power, seen in spiritual gifts of healing and power over demons. As a result of proclamation, new communities of believers are to be formed within towns and cities. These communities will be often persecuted, rarely powerful politically, but are to act as salt does in meat and to be a sign of righteousness.

Unmet needs

I began to ask questions and discovered that official and unofficial estimates of the squatter and slum population range from 1.8 million to 3.6 million — thirty to forty per cent of Manila's population and growing at a rate of twelve per cent per year.

We found ten evangelical aid programs amongst these three million. A number of churches also had extension Bible studies into the slums. But of the more than four hundred missionaries living in Manila, to our shame not one was actually *living* amongst these poor. (A number of local Catholic priests lived amongst them.)

After eight years of searching, we have found just six Filipino pastors who have lived in these slums and established significant churches. That is one church for every 500,000 squatters — equivalent to one church for the whole of the city of Wellington, or just seven churches in Sydney. What further reason is needed for a life of proclamation and identification with the squatters of the slums of Asia?

Most Christian agencies to the poor had been captured by the social work concept: the basic issues are the economic issues, the entrance point is economic programs. One should only attach an evangelist to such programs, and have Bible studies for the recipients of the aid, after the economic need has been met.

This error of many evangelical aid agencies appears to be not so much theological as tactical. The entrance point into communities in the scripture is *not* aid programs, projects or good deeds. It is the breaking down of demonic powers by the proclamation of the cross. This is accomplished in the context of doing good deeds and results in spiritual change, which in turn transforms social, economic and cultural values.

It is because of their deep commitment to the proclamation of the gospel that the Salvation Army has had a fine balance between the social and spiritual. They see their social work as a pastoral component of ministry, and is only commenced (usually a year later) after the establishment of a local 'corps'. Even in community projects amongst the people, their workers always see Christian salvation as the priority. There is a vibrant passion for seeing people turn to God on the one hand, with the expectation of economic transformation following spiritual transformation.

It is essential for any disciple with a burning sense of mission to proclaim the kingdom. Economic programs may be added in any number of ways to such a person's work, but the power of proclamation is the essential starting point for any growth of the kingdom.

There is no question of spiritual versus material. The kingdom is holistic. But there is a definite set of priorities in effecting socio-economic-spiritual change within a community:

1. Proclamation leads to disciplemaking.
2. This in turn leads to pastoral issues.
3. These result in building a new social structure where economic needs can be discussed and enumerated.
4. This then involves dealing with politicians and seeking changes in public policy or political personnel.

What then of social work?

Social work and community development are, indeed, significant areas of Christian activity — to the extent that they are reflections of biblical teaching on social relationships, financial dealing and political action. As such, much of the work of the kingdom of God can be inter-related with that of government and private agencies working in the squatter areas. At the same time the kingdom comes violently (but not by violence!), so that its truth may at times create disharmony, where people persecute Christians for living and preaching the truth (John 15:18-25). This is seen as a violation of professional humanistic social work ethics.

Social situations

Having determined the primacy of proclamation, we still need to discern at which points to grapple with the broken social structure, inadequate economic opportunities, and the corrupt political structure. The following diagram shows some of the possible points of attack.

Classes of urban poor	Problems of the poor
1. Squatter areas (approx. 2 million)	1. Demonic influences: animistic/Catholic culture
2. Slum areas (approx. 1 million)	2. Illegal dwelling-housing
3. Families in other parts of the city below the marginal level	3. Unsanitary environment: * garbage * sewerage * water supply
4. Disabled and handicapped	4. Health and nutrition

5. Youth offenders, unemployed youth, drug addicts
6. Unemployed and under-employed, labourers
7. Exploited factory workers
8. Orphans and widows, prostitutes, marriages

5. Education
6. Under- and unemployed
7. Broken social structure:
   * indifference to neighbours
   * gang warfare
   * early and illegal
   * broken families and immorality

Some points at which to fight against poverty

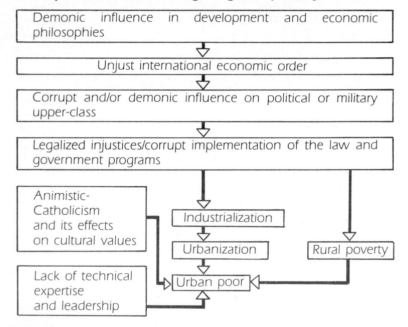

Which need?
The following is a brief review of some of the problems of the urban poor.

1. Demonic influences of an animistic/Catholic culture
The continued heritage of animism, the continual appeasing of saints and spirits — even God himself — is in direct contradiction of the biblical view of mankind, the ruler of God's creation.

Perceiving success as the blessing of the spiritual powers (or added graces from God) leads to a *bahala na* ('its up to fate or God or spirits') attitude that precludes preplanning, management skills and commitment to work with the hands.

Direct demonic control of individuals through the worship of the saints, use of curses, praying to the dead and other mediumistic practices results in much sickness, many handicapped and emotionally disturbed people.

Both areas are points of immediate offence for the gospel.

2. Employment

Basic to the meeting of most needs is the need for an income. A survey of 1,500 people in one established slum in Manila showed the following breakdown of occupations.

Occupations of employable adults in one established slum district in Manila (employable adults over fifteen)[3]

Unemployed (68% of total)	1,191	Shoe repairmen	6
Bar girls (hostesses)	105	Salesmen	6
Unskilled labourers	102	Govt. employees	5
Vendors	55	Bus conductors	10
Drivers	89	Stable boys	4
Dressmakers	40	Hairdressers	4
Waitresses/Waiters	30	Electricians	4
Barbers	10	Storekeepers	5
Manicurists	10	Masseurs	5
Laundry women	10	Hospital attendants	5
Gasoline boys	10	Janitors	3
Bouncers	10	Midwives	3
Scavengers	12	Mechanics	3
Tailors	9	Bakers	3
Carpenters	7	Policemen	2
		Butchers	1

Notice in the above (an industrial context) that the number of tradesmen consists of seven carpenters, four electricians and three mechanics — a total of fourteen workmen out of 1,500 or a mere 1% (assuming that all the above were in fact skilled). This demonstrates one of the critical needs: the introduction of practical trade skills into these communities.

3. Housing
The Filipinos call them 'squatters' which aptly describes the insecurity of the new city migrant. Too poor to purchase land and build a house within a reasonable time, unwilling to pay rent for decaying accommodation or perhaps unable to find a room for his own family, the migrant is impelled towards the illegal occupation of land. He becomes a squatter on land in dispute, unused public land or buildings, frequently flooded land or land beside railway tracks.

Third World communities have neither the money, nor the technical skills to mount a city housing program on the scale demanded by the recent immigration. Four approaches have been tried:
(a) the provision of housing estates which the poor cannot afford
(b) the practice of eliminating or ejecting the squatters *en masse* from their land
(c) the provision of sites and services — roads and services laid out, enabling the site owner to construct his own house
(d) the upgrading of existing areas over a period of time.

The third and fourth options provide some hope, but in most of these cities the absence of an effective comprehensive policy for housing the very poor reflects a preference for allocating scarce resources for the benefit of the richer classes. It appears that there are ultimately no solutions to this problem. The solutions that worked in nineteenth century Europe are no longer applicable. Present solutions and resources are inadequate. The problem will grow. Nevertheless, we must do all in our power to alleviate it.

4. Insanitary environment
The very illegality of housing means garbage collection, sewerage, water supply and electricity all have to be obtained illegally or informally. This results in frequent sickness. Malnutrition further adds to the sickness and death toll.

5. Education
Despite its availability, families can ill afford education for children. Working is the alternative to elementary school. It destroys any future of higher education or better employment.

6. Broken social structure
The uprooting of millions from their traditional provincial roots into an environment lacking the old social controls so important

Some of the pastoral team and believers celebrating

Henry, George and their extended family

Wherever land is available, squatters erect their homes —
often beside rivers and waterways

Drainage in Tatalon: open and above ground

Aling Lydia (left) leads a cottage industry of twenty women producing beautiful crocheted garmets — here modelled by herself and Corrie (right).

Recycling used cans, plastic and thongs (jandals) from the
rubbish dump

The squatter settlement of Tumbakan (by the rubbish
dump) and the local Protestant church — facing in
opposite directions!

in traditional and group-oriented cultures leads to an almost total breakdown of moral values, community and family relationships. Immorality, gambling and drunkenness run unchecked. Gang warfare is frequent.

7. Home of the destitute
These areas also become the final dwelling place for the failures, the outcasts and the drop-outs of society. The widows, orphans, deaf, dumb, blind, alcoholic, drug addicted and all classes of misfortunate find the slum areas the only place to live.

8. Injustice, oppression, exploitation
In this context, prostitution and slavery occur, those who have work are exploited, corrupt politicians, land-owners, businessmen and others cheat the people and create deeper poverty.

9. The future
There is a possibility that this trend towards urbanization may slow down. However, the future shows no evidence of any solutions. These problems will grow.

It seems highly doubtful that many of the proposed measures of rural development will stem emigration from the provinces to the cities. The prevailing patterns of economic dependence of the Third World nations on the industrial nations will perpetuate and increase the social inequalities within the poor nations. Radical structural reforms may be difficult to bring to completion due to the status of dependency on the First World. The very scale of the problems appears to be beyond what most governments can cope with. Efforts are likely to be concentrated on a few areas to the neglect of the remainder.

The communities themselves will slowly change: the immigrants will be better educated than those of former decades, the proportion of second generation squatters will increase.

The state and para-state bureaucracy will not be able to create jobs for more than a minority of migrants or primary school leavers. Most will have to be absorbed into the informal sector, i.e. into small-scale labour-intensive activity, poverty and patronage, dependent on the formal sector, working long hours for low financial return.

Mobility through education is likely to be slight. So too, are the chances of upward mobility in the entrepreneurial sector.

Yet the people will continue to hope. The story of the local boy who has made good will have more influence than statistics indicating the improbability of success.[4]

Blueprint

The strategic question is: Which of these issues do we attack first?

The Lord has already over these months used the 'Framework of Development' paper to whittle away at the demonic influences in development philosophy. This paper had been passed on by friends to various professors, politicians and colonels who were using it to provide a Christian basis for development. But it seemed that the basis of any further strategy must follow Jesus' strategy. He, after all, is the head of his church and proclamation to the poor is his command — a command to attack at a direct spiritual level, to reach deep into the soul of the culture at the centre of poverty. Healing, miraculous signs, demonic confrontation and other spiritual gifts are all ingredients of the biblical account of such an offence.

The squatter areas were the logical places to begin, as all other classes of poor dwell there. Evangelism was the starting point.

It seemed wise to begin in areas where the National Housing Authority in its Zonal Improvement Programs had begun to deal effectively with upgrading housing.

After months of interaction with friends and co-workers, the time had come to put our thoughts on strategy into a flow chart for action. I worked for a whole day just trying the schematize the future directions of ministry if we would establish discipling movement amongst the bottom 12% of Manila's society, the one million poorest. I was excited, sensing I had on paper a strategy that would work. I ended up with two pages of flow charts and jotted down some guiding principles. Amongst them:

'Discipleship is the focal point of the ministry, not social work, nor creating a funding agency, nor skills training. Holistic discipleship involves both personal piety (the development of a spiritual relationship with God) and active involvement in the socio-economic needs of people. Only the Spirit of God can do this.'

I took these months of thought to my leader. He glanced at it and gave it back! I put it away in my drawer muttering to myself, 'I must have made a bad mistake. If God's going to do it, it will have to be his work and not my planning.'

A year later, I took out the plan for a friend, dusted it off and looked at it in amazement — for God had done what he had revealed. The twentieth step had *already* been reached! Such is the work of God! Two years later, the next phases, despite many traumas and problems, had occurred also. God is at work. God is determined to establish his work amongst the poor. May we be found faithful to sense his direction and fall in line with what he is doing.

Footnotes on Chapter 7

1. General William Booth, *In Darkest England and the Way Out*, Salvation Army, 1890
2. Paul Sabatier, *Life of St Francis of Assissi*, Hodder & Stoughton, London, 1907, p 118
3. Landa F. Jocano, *Slums as a Way of Life*, University of the Philippines Press, Quezon City, 1975, p 31
4. These thoughts on the future have been summarised from Peter Lloyd, *Slums of Hope, Shanty Towns of the Third World*, chapter 9, Pelican Books, 1979. Reprinted by permission of Penguin Books Ltd.

8

New Ministry, New Power
THE REALITY OF GOD IN THE SLUMS

THE TIME HAD COME. There had been sufficient time for reflection and sufficient structural analysis of the causes and issues of squatter poverty. The theological basis for mission to the poor had been developed. The Lord had given a strategy. But where was my companion from amongst my friends?

In Filipino culture, a high premium is placed on companionship. For many months I had been asking and praying for someone to join me in this work. All whom I asked were gracious in their refusals. Some had family obligations, some were too busy grappling with their own struggles or their own inadequacies, some were making money, others were earning degrees. Many had not yet fully considered the word of God about the poor.

One morning the Lord spoke again from Luke 14:

> But they all alike began to make excuses. The first said to him, 'I have bought a field and I must go out and see it; I pray you, have me excused'. And another said, 'I have bought five yoke of oxen and I go to examine them; I pray you have me excused.' And another said, 'I have married a wife, and therefore I cannot come' (Luke 14:18-20).

He was telling me to press on regardless of companionship. He would bring some of the poor to provide this:

> Go out quickly to the streets and lanes of the city and bring in the poor and maimed and blind and lame . . . For I tell you none of those men who were invited shall taste my banquet (Luke 14:21 and 24).

Choosing a community

For some months whenever I had free time I had leaped on a motorcycle and roved from squatter community to squatter community.

One day I rode down the narrow paved road between the old higgledy-piggledy houses of Santa Ana. Down the *kalyes* I could see acre upon acre of galvanized iron and plywood shacks, stacked one leaned against another. The children here were silent. No 'Hi Joe's' as in other places. There was spiritual darkness like the darkened colour of the old house. The iconed chapel on the corner gave a clue. Every house seemed full of saints. The sense of the demonic was very real.

There were several more chapels and, in the midst of all the squalor, a magnificent religious school.

'Hey Joe, where have you come from?' came the traditional greeting as I stopped by some older men.

'I'm lost,' I replied. 'I see you're having a fiesta soon.' I pointed to their decorations across the small main street.

They smiled and described the celebration to their saint and the Virgin. Santa Ana — the demonic squatter community. This was not the place to begin the work of God.

The next day, I wandered along a dirt road by a river. Many squatters live on the rivers, since this is where older *'barrios'* (small villages) existed. They were a nucleus for other poor people to congregate. The rich do not use properties that flood.

Around the community was mile upon mile of heavy industry. The children laughed at me as I passed. Their 'Hi Joe' was one of hatred and derision, not the wide-eyed, smiling banter of famed Filipino hospitality.

The men's faces were sullen and nasty. There was the noise of frequent family fighting. I quickly turned back from one street upon seeing knives drawn between two men.

A fit harvest

And then there were other areas. Amongst them was Tatalon. As I entered it, I saw people busy building. There was laughter in the backstreets. There were happy children. There was activity. There was a spirit of *hope*. Above all, the Holy Spirit impressed on me in his voiceless Spirit-to-spirit communication, that this place was one where he was at work.

Part of the reason for hope was the excellent upgrading program in this community. I have noticed that where economic progress is being made, people are more responsive to the gospel. Positive changes in one area of people's lives gives them a desire for further positive changes.

I spent some time wandering around the streets. The councillor in one area was loading scrap metal into his jeep. 'It's hard work that counts,' he said. *'Tiyaga, sipag!'* (Patience, industriousness!)

In one area of Tatalon, the upgrading program of the National Housing Authority was well advanced. People were busy building houses of concrete blocks. The sound of hammer and saw and the bustle of an active people was evident.

The councillor told me of a Catholic priest who had formerly lived there. I walked through the scrambled labyrinth of walls, picking my way across the mud and dirty water trickling along the lane and asked people where he used to live.

The family where he lived were most courteous. This priest had truly lived simply — a man given to prayer. But the military had come and he was deported. He had been involved in 'activism' against the government, fighting against the housing program and offending those *barangay* leaders who had been appointed by the Marcos government to lead Tatalon.

He and his companion had built a small chapel in which to say Mass, but then the National Housing Authority had pushed it down. It was illegal. He had become angry.

I went to visit another priest, a friend of his. He was a big, bearded, softly-spoken American. He told me the background more fully. Their objective was the building of a basic Christian community. They tried to do it by fighting for justice in the issue of housing and then by developing an education program. Both attempts failed. I sensed the powerlessness of a committed but inert Catholicism in his words as he described the time when the *barrio* captain had stood by as his companion priest was taken to prison for his work as a community organizer.

Did he know of any righteous people, any godly contacts in Tatalon? No, he did not. He advised me to live in another section of the community to that in which he had struggled. Perhaps there would be more success there.

Georgina was one of thirteen social workers in a Bible-study group in the National Housing Authority. She volunteered to take me into the community to introduce me to the community leaders and discuss my desire for a home from which to minister spiritually to the people. Three weeks later I was busy cooking in Aling Nena's upper room.

At home at last

As I cooked my rice and fish on the little gas burner and boiled my water (as I always did), I mused on how to incarnate Christ in this community.

If I was to be the incarnate body of Christ in Tatalon, I must not only dwell there, but let the character of Christ reveal itself in me. I must love. I must give of myself.

But I alone could not incarnate God. I am but a *part* of his body. I quietly prayed as I ate that God would bring me co-labourers.

That evening two of my former team members came to help me clean my house. Outside the lightning and thunder flashed and roared. We put plastic over some of the holes in the walls to keep out the tropical rain that pummelled furiously on the roof. I had rescured the cardboard that had come around a friend's fridge, so we used this to line another wall. The average kill per day was ten cockroaches in this house. (The occupant of the next room upstairs killed 98 one day — her children counted them! She used up a whole bottle of insect spray I had bought!) To complete the arrangements, I hung sacks around the inside of the windows to keep the rain out between the cracks. We were careful not to disturb the lizards that lived there. They fed on mosquitoes and other insects. They are friends.

That evening sitting in my window, I thanked God for providing a centre and a home for reaching Manila's poor. My evening prayer was, 'Lord, I need a comfort room (toilet) so I don't have to share with twelve others. Otherwise I will get sick.'

As I was scrubbing next morning in my shorts on my knees with a bucket of water, I heard a shout, 'Viv! Viv!' from down the three-step ladder (each step being eighteen inches high) that served as a staircase to my mansion. Liza, the little seven-year-old from below came up the stairs to my room. '*Si Aling Aging*' (It's Mrs Aging), she smiled shyly at me. I poked my head out the hole above these steps. It was the happy face of Aling Aging, the barrio councillor.

I climbed down into the mid-morning sunshine.

'Would you like to use our extra comfort room'? she inquired with her normal bouncing laugh. (Her husband was a seaman, which is the top economic bracket amongst squatters. They earn dollars!)

I laughed back, 'Is there a spare one?'

'Yes, we have one we don't use. We dug our own at the house.'

I laughed again, 'I was praying about it last night.'

'Come over and fetch the key from Boy' she said, moving on to visit other houses in the cluster. 'We want you to feel at home. We can't afford for you to get sick.'

I nodded again, trying to catch the poetry of the Tagalog words.

I finished cleaning, thinking to myself, 'It's quite logical to walk in the steps of the labouring Carpenter.' The song kept running through my mind:

Love was when God became man,
Left his timeless place,
Dwelt in time and space.

God's incarnation is wrapped in compassion. He saw the unmet needs in the midst of his people and so came.

Reminded of carpenters, I walked across the dusty area outside our house, across the road, past the fourteen toilets all in a row to a carpentry shop that made cheap furniture for squatters. I met the owner and bought some plywood and nails. Two children helped carry it back, and I began to put a ceiling under the smoke-blackened and unbearably hot iron roof of my new home.

Fit for a king

How do you describe a squatter home? It had been built after the model of provincial houses, with good solid corner posts. Over the next few months the floor sagged in the middle a good four or five inches, but it was generally well-built.

Nerio came up the stairs to help me finish the roof. He was an expert carpenter and lived downstairs in another quarter of the house with his second wife. After working on the roof, we sat down and had a Pepsi together. He told me about himself — a man skilled yet impoverished by broken family relationships. As we talked, my mind was constantly concentrating on the Tagalog words.

One day I was sitting downstairs in Nerio's home and saw a rat running around the room where they slept. I threw a hammer and hit it mid-ribs. It leapt five or six times straight up in the air about two feet and then struggled into a hole. The people didn't comment. Later I discovered that one does not attack rats because they come back and attack you.

Rats kept me awake in my own room the first night, so I bought a rat trap. We caught three of them the next day. But they also provide humour. One night in the kitchen where I had put up the ceiling, I heard the rats start at the top and then zoom all the way down to the bottom of the sloping ceiling. Then they chuckled and chattered to themselves, climbing back to the top to zoom down again.

I put the rubbish outside in a little can that was hung from the house in a place where the rats couldn't get it. Old papers were given to Aling Nena. She used it in her little store to wrap up things for people.

Our next-door-neighbour washed my clothes for a few pesos each week.

The kitchen timbers were old and blackened with the smoke of charcoal fires over the years. The bench was made of a basin and bits of old wood. I used a two-burner gas stove running from a liquid petroleum gas tank. It was much more efficient than the charcoal or kerosene that most squatters use. Because of the cracks in the walls, I could look out to see what was happening at all times from my kitchen. The squatter area has electricity -most squatters tap the electricity off the power lines. Each night one usually went to the pump to fetch a couple of buckets of water.

I asked Nerio to make a decent table for the kitchen. He did it in a half day. This was where I would leave my typewriter. Coring from next door would come and type two or three days a week and I was able to find her a job typing for another missionary for the other two or three days per week. She had just graduated from a two-year typing course. So the kitchen also became a little office.

Windows were just vacant holes in the wall which we filled up with a piece of wood when it rains. This shutter swings on its hinges like a window at other times. In the six-by-ten foot bedroom was a desk borrowed from a missionary friend. Usually one slept with one sheet, on a mat under a mosquito net, rolling up the mosquito net each morning.

It is a strange thing becoming poor amongst the poor. First, you seek to live at their level — to do exactly what they are doing — and then, as you are doing that, you recognize and identify those things where you have physical or emotional needs whereby you can't live at the same level, so you make small adjustments.

That is acceptable to the people. Identification is not imitation. For example, I needed a good cassette tape recorder for language study. Most folk only had a radio. Also I needed a bookcase.

The houses for an incoming family would be about six-by-ten-feet and made of plywood with iron roofing. The older people in the community had put up larger houses which were equivalent to four of these small houses: two rooms upstairs and two rooms downstairs. There would usually be four families living in such a house. On the corner of our cluster of houses was one man who had become quite successful in engineering and had constructed a very attractive house. The lower storey had a concrete floor!

Often squatters live beside the railway tracks where there is some vacant land. Often roofs are covered with old tyres to hold the metal sheet on.

The best homes are raised off the ground which keeps them from the water and gives a little bit of privacy. Soon the bottom of the house is built in and new squatters move into that. Often they have relatives. The trees disappear quickly for firewood. Any vacant land nearby is very quickly cultivated to provide vegetables, since many of the squatters are from the province and still have agricultural skills. Perhaps one home in ten has a TV set. Such families may have someone working in an office job who could afford a TV. Everybody else watches the TV through the windows. It is an appliance that has to be shared.

Possessions are shared amongst the squatters, but one never enters another's home for a meal or during meal-time. One talks outside, lest the family be embarrassed and forced into buying extra food for the guest which they cannot afford.

Where does the wood and the timber come from for building the homes? Sometimes it is from plywood packing cases. Sometimes it is bought. For example, one day Aling Nena came back excited. She'd been out visiting a friend and there saw an old truck. She was able to buy the roof off the truck! This would make a good roof for the new *sari-sari* store she wanted to put up.

Life is a daily pattern. Early in the morning the teenage girls use their straw brooms to sweep the dust off the bare earth between houses. The mothers sit on their haunches washing in their basins, or washing and soaping their hair. Others, dressed beautifully, walk between the plywood homes under the washing, dodging the puddles, laughing at their friends and heading off for their work. The radios blare to waken the neighbours amidst a cacophany of shouting mothers and children.

The middle of the day is a time to keep out of the sun. Usually there is a siesta. Around three o'clock is the time for gambling. That is when the women have little to do. It is a good time for women's activities. Then, while they cook the rice everyone sits outside their houses to talk over the day's events as the sun sets. This is the time for friendship and evangelism.

God-sent overcoat

One thing was clear. Before one can effectively preach the gospel to the poor, one must know deeply the power of God. Before Jesus began his ministry, the Spirit 'descended on him in bodily form like a dove' and he became 'full of the Spirit'.

I deeply wanted to know that power of God. In the hunger and search for him, I had scavenged in an infinite number of the cracks and crevices of life. Now at the place of his call, my inner being, so much a desert, still hungered for that inner knowledge of God.

I knew that in obedience comes such knowledge:

He who has my commandments and keeps them, he it is who loves me, and he who loves me will be loved by my Father and I will love him and manifest myself to him (John 14:21).

It was clear, too, in the scriptures that in the choice of powerlessness he would display his power, in the midst of poverty he would reveal his riches, in the cross would be the resurrection, in brokenness would be power. For the Spirit of power is first a Spirit of fire, burning the chaff from our lives, burning out the dross of sin.

As I chose to direct myself in this way of poverty — of brokenness, of powerlessness — God was not slow to respond with himself in his own sovereign way.

He began to sensitize my spirit to his with a deep time of intense loneliness. For many folks, such a time comes before revival. For Jesus, it was forty days.

During those early days, loneliness not only walked with me: it hung like an oversized great coat. It had always been a friend, but now became my ever-present companion.

Friends amongst the professionals did not visit — some being too busy, some being afraid to enter the community, but most preferring to avoid the criticism of others who disagreed with any move into the slums. Some of the gossip was quite painful and eventually did much harm but, since it would have taken days of discussion to track down and deal with its source, I watched it multiply like a cancer and left it up to God's mercy.

Along with the feeling of aloneness, I felt Satan attack wave after wave. Fever lasted several days; I experienced an unpleasant rash; doubt and discouragement sought to overwhelm. The constant failure that is a normal part of any ministry and of culture shock continued.

During those first days in Tatalon, my thoughts could well have echoed Kagawa's simple words:

I came to bring
God to the slum;
But I am dumb
Dismayed
Betrayed
By those
Whom I would aid;
Pressed down
So sad
I fear
That I am mad,
Pictures
Race through my brain
And lie
Upon my heart
Pictures like this
A man
Legs rotted off
With syphilis
And yet
He need not fret
That money
Does not come
Because his wife
Is rented out
And brings
Sufficient sum.
One month in the slums
And I am sad,
So sad,
I seem devil-possessed
Or mad.[1]

Like Kagawa, I would love to have turned back but for the call of the One who loved me and who commanded:

No one who puts his hand to the plough and looks back is fit for the kingdom of God (Luke 9:62), and
My righteous one shall live by faith and, if he shrink back my soul has no pleasure in him (Hebrews 10:38).

Such statements were often the final motivation to press on into the darkness, the danger, the hatred:

> No friends, no companion, no ease or comfort, no position or power have I sought, none of these wanted. Yet, the poor are still far from me and so too is my distant God. I must yet go deeper into that cross. Somewhere in the fullness of his suffering he will meet me.

And God did! As the light fills and illuminates, so his light began to fill and to flood my life in the midst of darkness. Day by day I would spend some hours in the word of God and in prayer. In the midst of drunkenness, oppression and immorality, that love filled and cleansed me in a way I had never before experienced. There was renewing and a fullness of that power of God which began to radiate out to the destitute around. Those groups that I prayed for during that time were the ones who were later converted. God began to reveal his power.

As a child, I had experienced that overwhelming presence of the love of God as it flowed over and over me day after day. Often at times as I had been preaching, I had seen his anointing on his word. God's spirit would descend on people, but now he began to break forth with a new power and joy. There had been times when the spiritual gifts that he gives to us at conversion had been evident, but now there was a deeper sensitivity to him, a freer flow. A cleansing of old sin and traditions unleashed these gifts.

As a youth I had seen a pattern from reading hundreds of the biographies of the great saints. Somewhere ten-to-fifteen years into these men's ministries, they often entered into a deeper life, a new empowering of the Spirit of God. There were various terminologies, various doctrinal persuasions, some talking of 'Christ in me'. Corrie Ten Boom tells of 'entering his rest'. Others talk of the 'immersion of the Spirit', 'release in the Spirit', or 'the baptism of the Spirit'. Others speak of a continued series of fillings of the Spirit; some of the anointing of God.

It is good there is a diversity of doctrine on this issue for 'The wind blows where it wills and we hear the sound of it, but we do not know whence it comes or whither it goes, so it is with the Spirit.' God is not an abstract doctrine. He is alive and sovereign. He had met me and now began to move in new ways beyond my prayers and work. For long my ministry had been such a struggle, so dependent on *me*. Now I had difficulty keeping up with *him*!

Mind you, Satan was not weak in the counter-attack.

In counselling others on the secret of life in the Spirit, I have found no set formula. All I can do is point to the cross — to its suffering, to the obedience it demands, to the discipline it imposes, to the power of its proclamation, to its absolute authority.

Many Christians want power; few want holiness. Many want the resurrected life; few want the cross.[2]

The spirit world

One of the first evidences of a new power was in confrontations with demons.

In the slums one comes more and more into direct demonic confrontation. The Lord began to train me in this area, too.

One day I was doing some business in Makati, the rich city in Metro-Manila, when the Spirit of God began to speak to me very strongly. When that happens, one acts quickly!

I travelled back home. As I arrived, a leader in the ministry also arrived.

'Your engineer friend, Ra-ul, is calling for you. He is attacked by a demon.' We travelled quickly to the house.

Some days earlier, Ra-ul heard an evangelist who told him to 'listen to the Spirit'. He began to listen and, initially, what the Lord said to him was in line with the scriptures. But, as he kept listening, another spirit began to speak.

'God is light. The sun is light. Worship the sun.'

Ra-ul had thrown away his shoes, his wallet and his shirt under the instructions of this spirit before being picked up by the police. They called his wife.

The family were angry at Ra-ul for having read the Bible and hence getting involved with a spirit. But finally because the spirit gave him no sleep Ra-ul told them, 'Bring me over to the ministry centre.' There, they read the scriptures and prayed, but the spirit kept troubling him each time so he would stop praying.

When I arrived I didn't know what to do, so I asked questions to discern the background. Then I prayed commanding the spirit to leave. It would go, Ra-ul would begin to rest, and then back it would come — talking, talking, talking to him. We prayed again. I asked Naty, his wife, to begin to read the scriptures. Whenever she did, the evil spirit would depart again. She prayed to become a Christian. We told Ra-ul how to use the name of Christ against the spirit. After more prayer, it left without much of a fight.

His father arrived with a whole jeep load of people. Amongst them them was a man with sharp, piercing eyes who kept saying, 'You know there is somebody higher than Jesus Christ.' I recognized him as a medium. They had brought him to cast the demon from Ra-ul. We explained that he had been freed by prayer, the scriptures and the name of Christ.

The discussion lasted no little time. Finally, his father was happy with our suggestion that in two days' time Ra-ul should return to the province where we would gather the neighbours and explain how he became freed. This would save the family honour.

Two days later we all travelled in a jeep back to the province. All the neighbours gathered. All the relatives gathered. There were people standing all around the windows looking in.

Ra-ul gave his testimony. Milleth sang and Pastor Jun preached. We talked till midnight. Many believed that day and the Lord wrought a great victory indeed, turning the tables on Satan.

My brother, the professor

God used my relationship with another close friend to give me a deeper understanding of how to grapple with the spirit world.

A few months before moving into Tatalon, I received a request from a friend to take over the follow-up of a professor and of a politician he was helping. Both were doing Ph.Ds at the University of the Philippines. I sensed that God was evident in this request.

The professor was the father of eleven children and professor of graduate studies at Isabella State University. He was a big man, a leader, a man of high standing amongst the Ibanag (Ee-ba-nag) people. His relatives were mayors and city officials. He was also a gifted orator.

There are 335,780 Ibanag people who live in and around the Cagayan Valley in Northern Luzon. They are a dignified and proud people, with a strong sense of identity and culture.

Until now, there has been no significant breakthrough for the gospel amongst the Ibanags since the initial thrust of evangelical Methodism in the early 1900s. God gave him boldness to invite first one, then three to a Bible-study group. The principal of the high school came to Christ. Others came.

A compassionate man, he saw a little sick boy, put his hand on his head and prayed. He was healed. This happened several times.

He came back to visit us in Manila. I sat with him and the soft-spoken research assistant who had led him in Bible studies. He shared his experiences and then asked, 'Do you think this is from God? Do you think God will take it away?'

We encouraged him and a month later took a team up to Isabella to run a three-day 'Dynamics of Christian Growth' seminar.

When I preached at his Bible study, there were seventy people attending. What a work of the Spirit of God! After the seminar, the four high school delegates went back and led one hundred others to Christ — almost their entire school.

But much of my brother's early life had been marred by cruelty. In his relationship to his own family, there was much of the scriptures to learn. My role was to be one of friendship and encouragement to build balance, character and depth in the word.

Late one night we sat up with him, as he poured out the terrible cruelty and pain and asked the Lord to heal each memory. He began to show love to his children, and God began to fully restore his relationship with his wife and family.

There were many defects, but the gospel moved so rapidly that, within six months, over a thousand Ibanag people had turned to Christ.

As a leader in the community, he was frequently invited by his relatives (often the mayors of neighbouring towns), to preach in their barrios or in the neighbouring chapels. (At this point the parish priest was positive towards the movement since he himself had translated much of the scriptures into Ibanag.) When he would preach, it would often last two or three hours. People loved the oratory in their own dialect.

One time we were invited by the director of the tobacco research unit to address his thirty workers during office hours. As time passed and the cross was preached, the men began to weep.

After the message, he would say, 'Now would all those who have not believed stand up.' They believed! Later the decision would be personalized, but in Ibanag culture, decisions are made in a group context!

Couples were reunited, drunkards released, people healed. In one weekend there were four encounters where demons were cast out.

The army officers of the province asked him to come and speak. He interpreted for them a biblical approach to development in their province, beginning with the gospel, beginning with spiritual and cultural liberation.

Why should God use a two-year-old growing Christian in such a dynamic way? The history of church growth illustrates that, when God wants to break open a tribe held long in animism, he will often choose one of the tribal leaders within the movement.

Then he will empower such a person to confront the spirit powers of the tribe.[3]

Missionaries have often failed to exploit such opportunities. Discipling movements must quickly follow behind such a response of people turning to Christ. Fortunately, the leaders within the *Lakas-Angkan* were sensitive to the Lord. We were able to despatch one of the key ministry leaders to assist the professor in consolidating and building a core team of people, who could disciple the new believers.

We kept encouraging him to remain within the Catholic framework. To move out would create a socio-cultural barrier and prevent the full consummation of the movement. But the public burning of idols created a wide rift, after which he came into direct conflict with the Catholic church in his preaching against idols and worship of saints.

Wisely his gospel message focussed around the difference between the biblical world views of spirits and the Ibanag world-view. In the Ibanag world-view, there are both good and bad spirits. The good spirits assist people to do good and to heal. Life is spent in appeasing these spirits. Despite the people becoming Catholic in name, this was still their world-view. The Catholic saints and the Virgin Mary were added to the pantheon of spirits that needed appeasing. The real break with Catholicism is the break with animism. And this occurs when the idols — the 'saints' — are destroyed. That is conversion!

Guerrilla battles spirits!

One situation that had bothered me as I was recruiting the team to come and assist in the slums was the demonic attacks on the family of Manuel.

I had a long talk with his father. He had been a guerrilla fighter during the Second World War and was now head of a technical university. Their family was one of the leading families of the province — a good, God-loving and important family.

He sat back in his chair and, as is the custom of older Filipino men when entertaining, began to tell us a number of stories. These were about his dealings with the spirits.

In the first he told how as an officer in the Engineers during the war, as they were making a road through the mountain prince, they came to a row of five trees. The first four trees required only a stick of dynamite to move them. But the fifth, after a single charge, did not move. They used a whole box of dynamite on it next. It still did not move. Finally they placed three boxes, the trees lifted up and flew horizontally to the ground several metres away, complete with the boxes. Two men who were assigned to dig under the tree struck the grave of a mountain king. Within six hours they died. He, himself, began to get a deep fever. He called his men to find the local witch doctor. The medium came, prayed for him and he survived.

At another time in the mountain province, he slept in a hollow, also a burial place of the mountain kings. The people warned them that nobody had ever been able to sleep there. He and his companion could not sleep. A dream returned to him time and again of some men trying to scoop them up in a net. In the morning he discovered that his companion had had the same dream.

I learned that Manuel's aunt was a medium. His father was a good man, a very devout Catholic leader. He devoutly read the scriptures. Yet true to the Ibanag world view, he considered many of these spirits as good and helpful spirits which enabled one to gain control over other evil spirits, even at times to heal the sick. Catholicism, after four centuries, had been powerless to confront the basic core of animistic beliefs of these people.

I took the professor over one night and they swapped stories about their dealings with the spirits. He explained the difference between the biblical world view (all spirits are demons except the Holy Spirit) and the Ibanag world view (spirits are good, but mischievous and need to be appeased).

Manuel's father told us how once his whole family had been gathered together and a spirit had taken over one of the brothers and spoken to them of the sins of the family.

We prayed with him, but there was no apparent revelation to him. Then we went up to Manuel's room and commanded the spirit to leave. Goose pimples ran up my spine. Our hair stood on end. The spirit appeared to have gone at the time, but a year later the family was still being troubled.

This family will only be free when, as a family, they completely renounce their dealings with the spirit world.

A warfare of rest

Not only did this continuing experience of 'Christ being my life', of it being 'no longer I, but Christ in me', result in power in proclamation and in dealing with demons. There has come an ever growing knowledge of 'the rest of Christ'. It is through experience of knowing that the risen Christ is working that we can quietly relax and watch him work — though at the same time we may be all action, too. It is a quiet confidence that not only is he working, but that he will bring everything to successful completion.

People ask: In the midst of so much poverty and suffering, how can one cope with all the needs? The answer is we don't have to. That is God's task!

I used at times to be so fearful that I would travel in the jeepney right past the squatter community, then travel on for several minutes until I had been able to review some of the passages of the scripture that gave me promise of God's protection, such as Psalm 121:8:

> The Lord will keep you from all evil. He will keep your life. He will keep your going out and your coming in from this day forth and for evermore.

Then I would get off the jeepney, get another jeepney back and walk in past the people. Always they seemed to be reaching out to be talked to, to be ministered to, to be loved. I didn't have the finances that they needed, so I would retreat within the poverty of myself. Yet as I would walk in with these promises of God fresh in my mind, he would direct me to which needs to meet. There was a quiet confidence that God was at work and was sufficient for the needs that he wanted me to meet. Perhaps here is where I fully glimpsed Calvin's emphasis on election. We do not have to meet the world's needs. God, the Holy Spirit, will choose people's needs for us to meet.

The fear would be replaced with quiet confidence and trust in the all-loving and almighty Father. In this is rest.

And God did protect. Only one person ever got angry with me in the community. One day I was talking with a mechanic friend who had constructed a three-wheeled motorcycle. He offered me a ride.

A drunken bystander on the footpath called out and asked me to take him with me. I did not hear. Later, when I came back, he came over and began to talk with me. He was angry. I could not follow his Tagalog. It was too intense, so I did not realise how angry he was. Kid, my friend, stepped in and quietened him down.

Later that afternoon this drunken man took that same motorcycle and smashed it. He knocked himself silly with concussion for the next two months. Fear came on the community!

All the people in the barrio said it was because God was protecting me, since I was his servant.

I knew that it was God, for that morning he specifically spoke to me of his protection from Psalm 91:

> Because he cleaves to me in love, I will deliver him; I will protect him, because he knows my name.

Some time later we prayed for the full recovery of the one who had been my attacker. In many incidents like this I discovered the literal truth of the ' Apostle Paul's words: 'For we wrestle not against flesh and blood, but against principalities and powers and spiritual wickedness in heavenly places', so that 'the weapons of our warfare are not physical weapons of flesh and blood' such as the weapons of the businessman, the politician or the church dignitary, 'but mighty before God for the overthrowing of strongholds'. God has not yet chosen to heal him.

Footnotes on Chapter 8

1. Toyohiko Kagawa, *Songs from the Slums*, SCM Press
2. A scholarly historical and doctrinal survey of views about revival is given by Richard Lovelace, *Dynamics of Spiritual Life*, Paternoster, 1979. Andrew Murray in 80 pages of notes at the back of *The Spirit of Christ* gives the most comprehensive biblical theology of the Spirit capturing both Reformed theology, Keswick theology, the influences of the Welsh revival and his own insights from the centre of the South African revival.
3. A motivating book on this principle is by Alan R. Tippett, *People Movements in Southern Polynesia*, Moody Press, 1971.

9
Breaking the Poverty Cycle
PREACHING THE GOSPEL TO THE POOR

I HAD BEEN IN THE COMMUNITY THREE MONTHS, much of that time spent in praying. The time had now come to begin preaching, for the battle had been won already in prayer.

First, I needed to go up and visit the new converts amongst the Ibanag people, so I prayed for an evangelist to live in my house while I was away. Two days later, in answer to that prayer, I met Jun and Milleth Paragas. They came to get some counsel on a problem they had. We discussed their problem and I suggested: 'Why don't you stay in my house for a couple of weeks while I am away and look after it for me? That will give you time to sort through your problem. You can do some evangelism while you are here!'

Back in 1974 we had worked together in church planting. I had watched as the Lord gave, then developed, in Jun the gift of an evangelist. They discussed the proposal together and decided to stay. They have stayed ever since! Jun is a tough man of God, a Bible school graduate from a farming family. Milleth is a petite, charming Filipina — a trained singer and a joyful wife.

For the next two months we lived together in the same two cramped rooms until we decided to find them another house — across by the cliff above the polluted river that circles around Tatalon.

It was only one room. There was nothing on the floor, just mud. Mud smells, but outside, between house and river, was a large expanse of land twenty feet wide, ideal for children and ministry activities.

The fellowship of his sufferings

The first activity we did, after planting a garden on the land beside the house, was to lay concrete on the floor to get rid of the mud smell. The second was to build a small bench and then to buy a small gas tank and some pots for Milleth to cook with. I would pay for all the food as payment for Milleth's cooking for me.

These meals were times of deep fellowship together. It was as we ate our rice and fish for breakfast together and shared our struggle that I began to learn what Paul meant when he talked of 'becoming partakers of the fellowship of the sufferings of the gospel of Christ'. Each morning one of us would be discouraged. It was not easy for Milleth to live in such a community. It was not easy for Jun, either.

They had been moving up socially, status-wise, economically. To become a squatter was to become a nobody.

There was a day when Jun came in excited from his time down on the river bank, reading his Bible in the early morning sun.

'I've finally understood why we're living here!' he exclaimed. 'I've just read 2 Corinthians 9:8. You know what it says? "Jesus though he was rich, yet for our sakes became poor, that through his poverty we might become rich". '

Our breakfast became a communion meal where, together, we knew the cup of suffering and the bread of the broken body of Christ, as we uplifted one another. But it was a suffering with joy. James says:

> Count it all joy, my brethren when you meet various trials, for you know that the testing of your faith produces steadfastness, and let steadfastness have its full effect that you may be perfect and complete lacking in nothing (James 1:2-4).

Only this spirit of joy in suffering, this knowledge that

> It has been granted to you, for the sake of Christ, that you should not only believe in him, but also suffer for his sake (Philippians 1:29),

only this spirit can in all honesty invite others to the task of identification with the poor.

Frontyard Bible studies

We decided that on Sundays at four o'clock in the afternoon, as the sun grew cooler, we would go through the Gospel of John.

All morning we spent preparing songs and charts and inviting all the neighbours. As the shadows grew longer, about thirty adults and twice as many children brought wooden seats from their houses to sit around the blackboard. We sang.

The first day, I experienced a wonderful freedom to preach in Tagalog. We began in Genesis and worked through to Revelation, very simply portraying fourteen events through the Scriptures. With their Catholic heritage, the people could identify with each story.

As the cross was portrayed, a silence came on the group. The Holy Spirit was clearly convicting. Then, I showed how the Holy Spirit came to those who believed and repented.

The finale of the Scriptures began to capture their imagination. They saw what the return of Jesus would mean for the poor: how even now God was building them mansions, how justice would be done. And they delighted in such promises. Truly, the gospel is good news for the poor!

The Filipino personality has a romantic, idealistic streak in it and is easily captured by fantasy. Such a mind can perceive clearly dreams of the future.

But there were problems also of the now! Questions came. Somebody asked on behalf of Aling Nena, 'Do I need to give up my gambling if I am to go to heaven?' I threw the question back to the crowd.

Another now very interested, asked 'How do I know if I have the Holy Spirit?' One man asked, 'Do you mean that even a bad man who believes can have his name written in the book of life?' Joy is seeing the gospel penetrate the daily reality of people trapped by hopelessness.

The tide breaks
John the Baptist came preaching:

> If you have two shirts, give one to the person who has none (Luke 3:11).

Doing justice in such small things is the key to the preaching of the gospel. One of the professionals took John the Baptist seriously and sent some clothes. Through these we reached Kid. Kid was the chief drunkard. He was known as 'Number One' — a big man, a tough and yet a wonderfully sensitive, intelligent man. He had lost his wife a few years before and had never recovered. Instead he had turned more and more to drink. God used Kid to open the community to the gospel.

It began on Christmas Day. I invited him up to the house to give him a gift of some jeans given by our professional friend. He was drunk. Sitting on the small step between my kitchen and my bedroom, tears welled in his eyes: 'Nobody else gave me a present this Christmas.' He wanted to do something in return. We talked long and he told me of the terrors of being a drunkard. Finally, he invited me the next day to his home.

When I went, he was not there. He was drunk. Each day after that as I would enter or leave the community I would pass Kid. He would be with a different *barkada*, always drinking. He would call me over and then he would introduce me to his friends.

'This is Viv, Brother Viv. He's a missionary. He's a good friend. You are to look after him.' Then he would introduce his friends one by one and I would shake their hands.

Kid would say, 'He's going to have a Bible study with all of you.' We would sit and talk a little and then I would continue on my way. In this way I was welcomed to many homes in Tatalon.

Jesus-style evangelism

December 26 was our birthday (Pastor Jun and I were born on the same day). We asked the ladies next door to make sandwiches and *pancit* (noodles). We invited all the neighbours to come and join us in a birthday celebration. We sang and we ate. And all the children ate — simple *pancit* sandwiches and juice. We had a good time. Then I stood up and sang in Tagalog and gave my testimony. It was the best birthday I have ever had.

Jesus tells us about birthday parties:

> But when you give a feast, invite the poor, the maimed, the lame, the blind, and you will be blessed, because they cannot repay you. You will be repaid at the resurrection of the just (Luke 14:13-14).

That was also Jesus' style of evangelism — always feasting!

Isaiah adds to the theme by talking of a different model for fasting. A day of fasting is to wander around the streets of your city and go and find a beggar, a drunkard, an old lady or . . . (who are the poor in your city?) and eat lunch with them. The kind of fasting that God wants:

Is it not to share your bread with the hungry and bring the homeless and poor into our house; when you see the naked to cover him . . . then you shall call, and the Lord will answer; you shall cry and he will say 'Here I am' (Isaiah 58:7 and 9).

Fasting and feasting — Jesus' style evangelism!

Noisy neighbours

One of the first people to experience the gospel breaking the poverty cycle was Aling Nena.

One night I was woken by the men in the gambling den below my bed, arguing as to who would go home first. The one who had won a thousand pesos dared not go, lest he be stabbed by the others. Aling Nena was shouting. She wanted them to go so she could sleep. (Aling Nena ran the gambling den. She took a *tong* or a percentage each night. That was her income.) Finally they went: the winner first, the others some time later.

My diary for the next evening recorded the following: 'Today Aling Nena is drunk. She wants to drown out the arguments from last night. She drank all morning and now she's shouting at Eleanor her daughter. Eleanor shouts back. Eleanor left later in the evening to sleep in another house so as to be free from the argument. I prayed, 'Lord, bring Aling Nena to a knowledge of yourself, for I cannot cope with living above such a gambling den. I need more sleep.'

While I was away on a trip, Pastor Jun gathered the whole family and preached the gospel to them. A number believed, particularly Aling Nena. The gambling stopped, but without gambling she had no money, so she went back to her gambling.

We helped her to set up a small *sari-sari* store. A *sari-sari* store sells a little bit of food, a little bit of this, a little bit of that. She soon gave everything out on credit. Within a short while the capital was gone. Back to her gambling Aling Nena went.

In the cool shadows one evening, at the time everybody sits on their haunches and relaxes after a day's work, I talked with her about Proverbs 31: about becoming a godly woman, being an old woman who is respected for being a leader in righteousness in the community. She understood. She stopped her gambling and began to live to do right. She began to teach her children to do the same. Aling Nena was the key to a whole extended family; her friends were gamblers and powerful men throughout the community.

As we talked that evening her niece came and joined us. She was waiting to go overseas to work in Hong Kong and had been working as a shop assistant in a store. She spent all of her income to process papers to go and yet she had been waiting for months and months. One of the evils of the poor is the exploitation by these people — export agencies called recruiting agencies who make exorbitant sums for the trade in human flesh. It's all legal. Yet for Edith it was a wiser choice to seek to go to Hong Kong and earn dollars than to remain in the poverty in which she existed. Any hope is better than hopelessness.

Edith has a son. We talked about raising her son into a man of conviction, and how the Bible was central to building this inward character in his life since he had no father. She understood. She asked me for a Tagalog Bible. Her joy was great. She was the one who had given up her room for me when I first came. God had now returned that blessing!

I've often thought perhaps that this whole process of exporting labour be developed along Christian lines in the way William Booth had proposed in his 'In Darkest England and the Way Out', where he sought to export people to the English Colonies of Australia, New Zealand and South Africa. Should we not set up a Christian agency to do the same function, but to do it justly and honestly, without kick-backs, corruption, evil and slavery?

Edith is now in Hong Kong.

Drinking men's Bible study

Drinking with friends is a way to fill up the day and to drown out the sorrow, the despair and the lack of manliness inherent in unemployment.

As I would walk into the community along the road past the houses day after day, I would watch groups of men sitting around on benches, the bottles of beer and the small snacks that they would have shared between them. Those that had work that day would share their money in order to provide the drinks for that evening. I began to pray, especially for the drunkards that would sit out in front of our cluster of homes. As I would walk over to my toilet, where I would wash each day from a bucket, I would walk through this group of men and greet them, sometimes sitting with them and talking with them.

There was one man who was totally destroyed by his continual drinking. I cared for him, loved him, talked with him. Aling Nena rebuked me.

'*Bale wala iyon*' (He's worth nothing!), she said, telling me not to waste my time. But God cares for the drunkards. Through loving him came an entrance into the hearts of the other drunkards. Here is how God opened the way.

I came home late one evening. As I walked down the road, I passed numerous groups of drinking men. There was no fear. I had learned the hard lessons as a teenager of how to refuse a drink graciously while standing up against the drunkenness of New Zealand high school students.

When I clambered up the stairs to my room that night, I saw the men had gathered in the next-door room upstairs where another couple lived. They were all drinking.

I boiled up some hot water, made a cup of tea and went in to join them. We talked and joked. Then one began to question me, 'How do you know there is a God?'

In broken Tagalog, I told them my experiences of God. They listened. One or two got drunker and drunker.

'Are you a Catholic priest?'

'No, I'm a member of an order which establishes Bible studies and helps people come to a personal relationship with God. We help them apply the Bible to everyday life.' So we talked and talked till they were too drunk to make sense and I slipped off to bed.

In this atmosphere it was time to establish rapport with the fellows. Later, we would talk with them personally when they were sober. Then I would build on this rapport and communicate the gospel more clearly. This is the kind of evangelism Jesus enjoyed: to bring the kingdom to drunkards, to set them free.

Murderer!

Several people were killed in the community in which I lived. I would avoid one track home at night, because there had been several murders there. I remember the day I talked with a murderer.

I was out talking with the drunkards. We were sitting on some benches they had set out in the sun on the dry earth between the houses. This area did double duty as meeting area, children's playground and a place for hanging out washing. I began to talk with a stranger, a friend of theirs. We got to talking on religious topics. There was some friendly give and take, as I sought to lay the groundwork for further sharing.

Gary, the new Christian, came over to me afterwards.

'Be careful with that one. He is a professional killer. You know the shooting you heard last night. . . ?'

'Thanks, Gary, I didn't realize that!' I was humbled again at God's protection. By his grace I had spoken gently to my murderer friend.

Proverbs tells us, 'The violence of the wicked will sweep them away...' (Proverbs 21:7). Many are swept away into the slums. Poverty is an environment for murder.

An old guitar

Often I would wonder why there was so little music from a people who are so musical. I noticed a lack of guitars, so I bought a guitar that I could lend to a group of drinking men who sat outside. (At least music is better than drunkenness.)

One half-destroyed young man would come and ask for the guitar. I trusted him with it. I was one of the few people who had trusted him. He considered this a high honour. Always he returned the instrument.

I began to pray particularly for this group of about fifteen drinking men. I would smile at them, love them and wonder how we could introduce them to a Bible study.

On New Year's Day I came back from celebrating with the staff of the mission group to which I belonged. It was early in the morning, the mist still about the river. The men had stayed up all night and were still singing songs. They wanted to make a tape for Junior, so he could sing to his wife. She was working as a maid in Hong Kong, sending money back to Junior to support him. They had no tape recorder, but that didn't matter! So they were sitting singing Filipino love songs.

Sitting down to relax with them, I asked them, 'Might I sing you a love song from New Zealand?' I began to sing 'Po Kare Kare Ana' (a Maori love song) and one or two more, then a Filipino love song. We had a grand time. They brought some food to eat. I sat with them enjoying the dignity and hospitality characteristic of Filipino people. I asked, 'We would like to have a Bible study with you guys, drinking men only!' They responded to the idea with a lot of humour! Pastor Jun joined us and we discussed the idea. The consensus was that we would meet at seven o'clock on Sunday morning before anybody drank. They could not join the study if they had already drunk! Pastor Jun would give the necessary leadership to such a group — my language was not yet fluent enough.

Thus began our drunkards' Bible study. We learned that drunkards do not enjoy a nice polite intellectual discussion about the word of God. They wanted us to teach them. So we would use all the authority and teaching skill we could muster. After the teaching, there would be discussion as to whether what was said was true and debates regarding its application. These men cared for each other. If one could not grasp what was being said, the others would teach him or would argue with him until he understood and believed.

A few weeks later I was walking down the concrete path carrying my little bag from a teaching trip to the province. I felt a hand reach out and shake mine, 'Hello, brod'.

I looked into a smiling face. It was Gary. My mind searched its files vacantly, desperately trying to understand the hidden meaning in these words, fighting hard to protect itself from another culture shock.

A second man joined him, smiling too at my confusion.

'Can you get me one of those Bibles, the easy-to-understand one?' I laughed mightily, enthusiastically shaking the hands of my new brothers. While I had been away, Pastor Jun had set up an evangelistic meeting to which 400 people came. These men had entered the kingdom of God.

The kingdom had come to Tatalon.

Our cathedral

We grew to love our cathedral in Tatalon. Our cathedral is magnificent, with its beautiful blue roof a hundred miles above us and God's dusty patchwork on the floor. We have air conditioning for, as the wind blows where it wills, so the Holy Spirit does the same amongst us. Our overhead transparencies are a large sheet of four-by-eight-foot manilla paper with songs written on them in Tagalog. The preacher's lecturn is a notebook in his hand. The comfortable pews with their cushions are the wooden benches brought from each house by the people to sit on.

But in our cathedral, God is there in a way I've rarely known in some of the architectural monstrosities elsewhere, travesties of God's creative imagination. Emmanual — God with us, God who dwells amongst the poor. We determined not to waste money on a church building. If we ever constructed a building, it would be related to vocational training or socio-economic development.

Emerging fellowship

From this point, the fellowship of believers in Tatalon began to grow. The story of its continuing development needs to wait for another book. The story from here on is not my story, but that of my co-labourers, Jun and Milleth. But let me outline its main thrusts.

Just as Jesus sought to identify with the cultural role of a scribe, so I had when possible sought to identify with the culturally accepted role of a priest, as a 'brother' in the movement which has Bible studies to help people come to know God.

There were two main thrusts to this ministry. The first was the Bible studies with the *barkada*, the groups of unemployed men and their drinking companions. The second was Bible studies to extended families.

We delayed baptism and distinctly Protestant worship, since we desired to work within the Catholic Church for as long as possible, in order to avoid a social and cultural dislocation.

Baptism or worship services are seen as Protestant activities. Baptism is not seen as a symbol of conversion from sin, but as a symbol of conversion to Protestantism. Thus, we also delayed baptism in order to maintain open links to non-Christian Catholic folk until there were believers in each segment of the community.

Rather than assembling folk for worship, we would have fellowships once a month, each creative and broad in approach, but gradually drawing together the Christians into a sense of identity — not within a Protestant church, but around the Lord they worshipped.

Discipleship and training in evangelism developed from the worship here. Often young men would oscillate between prayer meetings and drinking sprees until, step by step as we met with them morning by morning in 'group quiet times' (times of prayer and Bible reading), they would come to deeper commitment.

I wasted a lot of time seeking to develop Tagalog materials for the Bible studies, only to realize that the culture of the poor is not a reading/studying culture. We needed to work directly from the Scriptures.

This was illuminated for me as I was sitting with some young men, an old man and his granddaughter under the light set up outdoors in the cool evening breeze. We passed out some Bibles. Pastor Jun was teaching. 'Please excuse me, I forgot my glasses,' mentioned one (Filipinos are often indirect in their speech). We all smiled. A young girl was assigned to be group reader!

The critical element in terms of materials was to develop a consistent leadership training manual, rather than grass roots Bible studies. Despite not being able to read well, people devour comics. Comics cost only one peso each. I asked the Lord for the personnel to develop the Bible into comic form. A friend began to help with money available from a businessman, but my leaders rightly advised that the whole project was beyond our capacity at the time.

How could we provide Bibles for the poor? Whole Bibles cost 38 pesos ($US4) — a small fortune for the poor! We were expected to give Bibles. If we sold them, people would become suspicious that we were using evangelism as a money-making venture. We tried numerous ways of overcoming this barrier, but until now we have found no solution except to give or sell them at a small sum.

The coming of the middle-class

The believers multiplied. Over a period of several months, one by one God led middle-class friends to the area. They came saying 'God has called me to Tatalon'. One such was Theresa. If she hadn't responded to the call of God to the poor of Tatalon, she would have been completing her Masters degree in Manila's top management school.

Instead, here she was killing cockroaches! Killing cockroaches takes time and this worried her top-flight executive mind for there were twenty details to be accomplished in finalizing an export link-up to New Zealand, in completing an audio-visual on the squatter ministry and in assisting a new missionary friend to adjust.

I had received a vision concerning her — how she would choose between a lonely pioneering life in the slums, or a rich man in marriage. After a few weeks of working together, I told her about it. She told me her story. 'I was moulded for many years by my boyfriend. He was not a Christian and I knew our relationship was wrong. Finally, I broke it off. That is the rich man. It was after this that God called me to the slums.' God had been speaking and that is a difficult thing to ignore — not to mention the more immediate voices of the team cheering her on!

Theresa was the first woman (after Milleth) from the middle-class to venture to stay for more than a few days in Tatalon.

Worship

Around the room one Wednesday sat a band of highly intelligent, committed professionals involved in prayer and planning. The first phase of the work was almost complete. God had brought a ministry team together. After two years, the Lord had sent a number of these professionals to give their lives to developing a discipling movement amongst the poor. And sitting beside them in worship were now a band of young Christians, of whom some were taking leadership roles.

Johnny, a salesman and graduate of the University of St Tomas, one of Manila's top universities, had a gift of praying for the sick. And God heals through his prayers.

Resty delighted before the Lord in praise, reminding the Lord of the great issues facing the country, asking that he might be faithful to his call to poverty and begging for success with the economic projects God had gifted him to develop.

Pastor Jun Paragas took up the same theme with the Lord, his prayer reviewing the call, the costs, the sacrifices for each one, asking God to extend and develop the next steps in evangelism, praising him for new found patterns of worship.

Brother Romy, the engineer, prayed quietly, logically — the strong, silent structural thinker, of whom God had spoken prophetically as a church-planter.

Ofilia added her requests for the medical team she had been organizing.

Young Bien, whom the Lord had shown going through deep suffering in years to come, lifted his heart in adoration for the Lord's encouragements to him.

Luz thanked God for showing her his love when her fiance was far away. She had come for training in preparation for a married life amongst the rural poor.

Milleth worshipped before him in words reflecting the music of a soul deeply sensitive to him, thanking him for giving us the Tagalog songs we had been searching for.

Emy, the brilliant five foot tall theologian (was Paul like this?), was away on ministry to students. We prayed for him. Two years before he had been unable to come and join me, because of caring for his family. But God had not been still in his life. Finally he wrote the most beautiful letter to his church requesting them to release him for a ministry to the poor.

We began to pray for the coming weekend's activities.

The battle

It was an unusual weekend. Mang Ekyu had just begun to climb into a tricycle when, from inside the tricycle, a blade flashed. He felt something warm by his stomach, as he fell back and the attacker pushed past him. Blood!

'Quick,' he told the tricycle driver, 'get me to the hospital.'

Saturday night we sat by his bed as he told us his story. He spoke some English as Sally and Euan, two New Zealanders on two-month cross-cultural trips, were with me. A few days before, I had given his wife a cassette recorder and some tapes of Tagalog songs and the Gospel of John.

I talked with him about Lazarus and the rich man, and the two ways that men go. 'That's right,' he replied. 'If a man is good he goes to heaven; if he is bad he goes to hell. You know, I have not been to church for many years. The reason is this. When is child is baptised, you pay the priest! When you get married, you pay the priest! When you die, you pay the priest! But what if you are poor?'

Jun and Milleth arrived, opportunely to complete sharing the gospel. I accompanied Sally back to Valenzuela — two hours across town. (Women do not travel alone in Filipino society, especially at night.)

I arrived back home at 10.30 p.m. Resty and Emy had been waiting for me since five o'clock, to discuss the theology of poverty. I felt a failure, as I had been unable to provide the necessary hospitality and it was their first time in Tatalon. We rolled out our sleeping mats and mosquito nets. They slept, while I spent some time preparing for the worship time and the seminar on disciple-making.

Worship was at 8.30 a.m. It was free-flowing. We prayed and sang. Milleth sang as we prayed. Another sang his testimony and wept. The presence of God was felt so strongly that one young Christian began to confess his sin, and a drug addict prayed lucidly to give his life to God before the power of the drugs took over again.

Each week, one of us would preach. Deeply burdened, I preached for an hour.

Willie entered. He was deeply upset. The four of us growing into eldership roles sat silently. As we did so, Johnny saw in his mind a picture of a gun. He asked Willie, 'Do you have a gun?' Willie was startled! How did Johnny know? He began to share. The night before he had been drinking with our friend Kid. Kid was so drunk, he would not accept Willie's refusal to drink. He began to curse him and put him down.

But Willie was not unused to violence. He went to Tondo and fetched a gun and bullets from his brother. Never before had he been that close to murder. He was angry! We talked and joked until the passion had died. He went home and fetched the bullets and gave them to Johnny.

Johnny was now in a dangerous position, as possession of bullets could be interpreted as subversion. He took them and threw them in the river. We joked about it, for the week before Johnny had had a dream of being in prison with some of the new believers. Perhaps prison would be sooner than expected!

Just then a young believer came in. He was escorted by Mario. His eyes rolled and his body twisted — he was either drunk or possessed. As we prayed for Willie, he joined in. Then in tears, he told us his story.

The night before, while drunk, he had attacked his family with a *bolo* (a large machete). Fortunately, nobody was killed. He was still drunk, so his prayer was a quotation of scriptures that he knew. Gary had been the first to turn to Christ. He had never fully renounced his drinking. This day was the turning point in his life — the point of total commitment to Jesus Christ. From this day he followed the Lord wholeheartedly.

By this time it was lunch time and we had used up our discipleship training time in counselling.

We were being invited to a feast, to celebrate the baptism of Frank's one-year-old boy into the Catholic church. Frank, Kid's brother, was a new Christian. We took Willie with us.

Frank's place had plate after plate of delicious Filipino foods — hundreds of pesos' worth. We enjoyed a great feast. His sister Fe was the cook. We had had a Bible study at her new house the week before, after she had the priest bless the house.

We came back to plan with the team four events: the carolling, the Christmas party, Pastor Jun's birthday and the dedication of their child. The worship time was primarily for the leaders. These celebrations were a gathering for all believers.

The team then headed out to lead various Bible studies. I stayed back with some of them to teach them principles of leading a Bible study.

Confrontation with demons

Johnny returned with Emy. Emy, after two years of studying the theology of poverty, was flabbergasted! None of the standard theological books talk of being face-to-face with demons! Johnny had been praying for the health of each member of Willie's family. As he did so, he laid his hand on each one's head. When he came to pray for the girl who worked as a helper for the family, his hand was flung back by some powerful force from the girl's body. The girl ran screaming from the house, hair standing on end. We asked around and learned that her mother was an *albulario* — one who heals the sick by herbs and spiritual power. She did not want to be released, so we did not pursue it. One does not go hunting for spirits!

This was the fourth direct demonic encounter within as many weeks. The way in which the demons spoke showed clearly their fear of us — and their knowledge of how the word of God was being preached throughout the community. Breaking the poverty cycle requires a breaking of these demonic powers over men and women.

Jun and Milleth, in taking on these demonic powers, had themselves come under severe demonic attack. Milleth had been hospitalised twice; Jun had been in a motorcycle accident; Jedidiah, their one-year-old son, had contracted measles. It was one thing after another!

As we prayed together about this one night, I had a picture in my mind about an idol about bed height somewhere in the house. I asked around to discover where it was. The couple in the room next door had a whole gallery of them! Since their child had often been attacked, they had called in the local priest to cast out the spirit. He had blessed the saints instead! The couple eventually left the room to save their child. They left it locked!

We prayed against these and 'bound' them in the name of Christ. After this, Jun and Milleth were freed from the attacks. Jesus tells us, 'Do not enter a strong man's territory unless you bind the strong man.' We need to be wary of entering communities where Satan has focussed his power, unless we are able to bind those powers in the name of Christ.

The gospel is spread today just as in Jesus' day:

So they went out and preached that men should repent. And they cast out many demons, and anointed with oil many that were sick and healed them (Mark 6:13).

Another new believer also had a spirit within him. Some years ago a Catholic priest gave him a *mantra* (a word or series of words with spiritual power) in Latin to use against enemies, to obtain women and so on.

We needed to pray for his release.

Deliverance was coming to the community, but Satan was also

a kicking, fighting antagonist who would not lie down. Usually on Saturday evenings before a day of such ministry, he would attack violently with sickness. On Sunday evenings strange events would occur in our small house. But he was never victor.

It was now about six o'clock one Sunday evening. My *inaanak* (God-son), arrived. He is now a qualified engineer, whom God had touched with a desire to develop economic projects for squatters. The rest of the economic projects committee assembled in the large room Jun had built on to the house to house the vermiculture (earthworms)! While they were multiplying, we used it as a lounge.

After this I had supper with Melly, Jun's sister, and Evan, my visitor from New Zealand, who needed a little companionship after a day in an environment where he could understand little. I left him relaxing with the piano accordion that had arrived with some boxes of goods from my church in New Zealand.

It was late, but I heard that Aling Nena was in hospital. Should I go and find out what was wrong, or wait until tomorrow? I went back to my room and sat and prayed. James came to mind:

> Religion that is pure and undefiled before God and the Father is this: to visit orphans and widows in their affliction (1:27).

But since it was past nine and my body and emotions were past it, I decided to sleep. I hitched up the mosquito net to keep out the rats, cockroaches and mosquitoes and slept the sleep of the just, disturbed only by a rat knocking a jar into our rice pot and by the joyful sound of a group of midnight carollers next door.

My dreams were sweet ones. Two years ago, there could not be found a righteous person in this place. Today there were a number. Because of their prayers, the Lord might yet save Tatalon.

Could it be he would fulfil our prayers for a movement of 1,500 to 15,000 squatters firmly established in the word of God?

10
'Am I My Brother's Keeper?'
EXPERIMENTS IN ECONOMIC DEVELOPMENT

You are not making a gift to a poor man... you are returning what is his... The earth belongs to all, not to the rich.

St Ambrose

I SKIPPED OVER A MUD PUDDLE and flicked open my umbrella in deft Filipino fashion as the heavy rain spots began to crash on to the roading.

Aling Cynthia was just ahead of me, so I shouted out to her, '*Saan kayo papunta?*' (Where are you going?)

'*Sa trabaho! Ikaw?*' (To work! And you?)

'*Sa doktor*', I showed her the skin rash on my hands and feet that had developed from bacteria in the polluted pump water. We walked and talked.

'You know, Viv, you have no problems...'

'*Akala mo!!*' (That's what you think!), I thought to myself.

'...You have enough to live on.' Since Mang Mario her second husband had a heart attack, everything had gone wrong. 'You know how happy I used to be. Now I do not smile. For one year now, life has been so hard.'

I remembered Aling Cynthia as the enthusiastic member of a Bible study group a year before. I laughed to break the sadness. 'If only there was work,' I said.

I knew she would be forced to go to prostitution to feed her three children. We walked in the silence of sympathy. She knew that I knew.

'Yes,' she said. 'For one year now I have searched, but there are no jobs.'

Inside of me I felt as if my heart was falling apart. My mind flashed back to my conversation with a super-spiritual rich kid in a church back home, who had asked, 'Is it true you can just pray and God will provide jobs for people?'

I had simply told him, 'Yes, I can pray and God will answer. His answer is you. You are to sell all your excess things, work hard and make enough money to give to developing work for these poor!'

'Oh, Cynthia,' I said, 'I will do all I can. You pray for me, too, that I can find some men who will set up industries here in the squatter areas. It is so hard.'

Prostitutes need Jesus Christ — *and* an alternative income.

The drumbeat

There is a drum-beat, beat, beating in my head day after day, a beat that impels me forward into long hours of discipline and constant work. It is the cry of those saved from their sin, only to be entangled again by that same sin — by the tentacles of their poverty, drawing them down, down, down, till they are totally lost to this earth. We must work, must direct our undivided energy and unflagging zeal to the provision of economic stability for these, our new brothers and sisters in Christ. We must not be so busy working amongst the slum people that we forget to deal with the problems of the slums themselves.

Frank read the Tagalog Old Testament in three weeks after he was converted. He had time — he had no work. He was hungry for God. But without work and sitting around all day, the pressure of his *barkada* became too much. He returned to his drinking. Drinking men need Jesus Christ — *and* a job.

We must not only evangelize and establish churches; we must also pastor these new believers. That means we must establish industries, act as social workers and be reformers of the structures that create their poverty.

Exploited workers need Jesus Christ — *and* assistance in the right ways to relate to their oppressive employers.

Oppressive employers need Jesus Christ — *and* teaching on how to repent of their exploitation and ill-gotten wealth.

City officials need Jesus Christ — *and* models on how to repent from corruption and utilizing their offices for their own ends.

The deserted wife, the pregnant girl, the disillusioned prostitute, the aged and ailing widow, the hungry child, the underpaid mother working to support a fatherless family — all need Jesus Christ *and*. . .

'Evangelicals have always been rightly suspicious of mission boards that concentrate on education and medical, social, or economic ministries to the exclusion of or downgrading of evangelism and spiritual development. Yet, in most fields, there exists one or more of the following conditions which, if not attended to, will inhibit the development of independent churches.

'Where public education is absent, church planting must include education to enable members to read the Scriptures.

'Where sickness and malnutrition sap energies beyond the struggle for mere existence, church planting must include public health and nutritional services. . .

'Where there is just enough food to survive, church planting must include agriculture and related sciences.

'Where there is artistic or technical ability, church planting must include the development of these talents and where necessary the distribution of products.

'Where small businesses are possible and needed, church planting must include training in business practices and perhaps even financial help.

'The list could go on, depending on local conditions. In other words, in order to fulfil the church planting purpose of most missionary societies, a church planter must engage in more than evangelism and leadership training. Is it too hard a thing to say that it is criminal to go on establishing organized churches, condemned in advance to be permanently dependent on foreign money and personnel, simply because we neglect those factors in their society that make self-support possible?'[1]

The biblical response to poverty caused by sin is to preach the gospel to the sinner, but the biblical response to sin caused by poverty is to destroy the curse of poverty. Only when Christ returns will mankind fully be restored to his rightful role but, wherever his kingdom and his righteousness take root on earth today, substantial restoration occurs and needs to be facilitated.

First steps
To an outsider, one area of need appears to be hygiene. The poor of Manila spend much of their income on highly paid doctors and on an exploitative, profit-making private hospital system. We invited our friend Alan, a doctor, to come and teach the people about worms. He spoke first on 'How to get rid of the worms from

your stomach', then Pastor Jun spoke on 'How to get rid of the worms from your soul'. Over 90% of the poor have worms. Simple consistent teaching on basic hygiene needs to be an integral part of any growing Christian community.

If your people die young, of what value is your teaching? One friend, a university lecturer, began to join us once a week. Each time she came, she would bring some herbal plants to add to the pot-plant garden behind Jun and Milleth's house. Then she was reassigned to the province. Milleth continued the scheme till she became pregnant and could no longer cope with the project. Within the folklore of the people, there are sufficient remedies from herbal plants for most complaints (including common colds) and sufficient to make up a nutritional diet.

The Philippine Government has done sufficient research on their growth, traditional uses and dosages. All that is required is to find some representative of the poor, with the stickability and desire to develop the model, plus someone to train such a person in basic horticultural technique. In time, we may expect to find such a man or woman.

Within any cluster of squatter homes there are sufficient walls and roofs to develop any number of window boxes or pot-plant gardens. The potential from such a project in terms of herbal foods, medicines, hair shampoos and oils is well-known in Western countries. In time to come, God willing, a small-scale industry could easily be developed. The need is a man or a woman with the vision, the stickability, the willingness to learn the culture and develop the project over ten to fifteen years.

Why ten to fifteen years? Because most economic projects fail. As with the herbs above, one expects to fail and fail again until success comes. One research study analyzing four hundred projects in the Philippines by both the Government and private sector concluded that only twenty-five of these projects were moderately successful. After discussions with experts in the field I concluded that the basic reasons for failure are personal sin and the inability of the poor to manage finances. The sins include being too proud to feed the pigs, too lazy to water the plants and harbouring bitterness towards a member of the committee handling the project. This is where the gospel and the word of God are basic to economic change. Spiritual and social healing provide basic ingredients necessary for economic success.

Rabbits are an interesting case in point. I tried three rabbit projects at three different stages, but came to the conclusion that they require too high a level of technology and management to be a sufficiently simple project to supplement the meat in a squatter diet. (This is apart from the fact that the word *daga*, rat, is also used for rabbit!)

Why? Small things are important: cleanliness, care in feeding, detailed records for breeding and feeding purposes. When one litter of four-month-old rabbits is killed for meat, some of the money is required to be kept for feed until the next litter is killed. To someone without experience in keeping money — whose income each day is always insufficient — such thinking is a new skill to be taught. This means the development worker needs to give close supervision. I could not.

Pig-raising illustrates the same problem. Many people raise pigs. But one constantly comes across pig-sties that are not being used. The reason? A fiesta, a marriage, or a catastrophe. The pig is used. The capital is gone. Amongst those who have grown in a 'culture of poverty' there is usually little differentiation between capital, business finances and personal needs. Time, patience, perseverance in learning the detailed thinking of such a culture are essential.

Diet is another critical factor for the squatters. I searched out a group of nuns, 'Sisters of the Good Shepherd', who had devoted their lives to developing suitable diets for the poor — nutritious diets within the incomes of the poor. Missionaries to the slums need to master these. Some need to teach them to others.

The diet of the poor is fish and rice — a diet greatly deficient in vitamin B as only polished rice is available. For this reason (apart from worms), many of the poor are anaemic. Gene Tabor early on had introduced the *Lakas Angkan* to brewers yeast as a cheap way of supplementing this deficiency. *Mung* (mongo) beans supplement the protein requirements, but are also deficient in vitamin B.

But such areas as diet and gardens, goats, rabbits and pigs do not provide an income. They merely supplement or maximize the use of available income. The critical area of need is to find work, stable work in an industrial city that does not have sufficient industry for its people.

The problem is not a new one. William Booth faced the same in London's slums a century ago. His solutions included matchmaking factories (from where we get the word 'safety matches', since they did not use the toxic, yellow phosphorous that caused death and sickness in many other factories), trade-training factories (an early form of sheltered workshop), farm colonies and exporting men and women (after some skills training) to outlying British colonies such as New Zealand. Booth unfortunately died before implementing the last program.

Strangely, our first problem was not employment for squatters, but to assist Pastor Jun in the task of becoming a self-supporting evangelist. It was apparent to both of us that any discipling movement in the slums could not afford to be dependent on foreign funding for its leadership. The squatter people needed a model of a pastor who, like Paul, was able to support himself with his own hands. The first project Jun attempted was selling school supplies (notebooks, pencils, erasers and so on) under contract to an aid organization working with 400 women in the community. This was a project that was full-time for three weeks before the school term. It provided enough income for three months. What was needed, however, was an *ongoing* means of earning an income. Continuing to sell school supplies was a possibility, but it was apparent that we would be selling to a community without money. There would come a point, as the community continued to develop economically, where this would be feasible, but at this time it was not.

We really needed a cottage industry with marketing possibilities outside of the squatters — amongst the middle-class or with an export market. So Pastor Jun and his neighbours together did a feasibility study of a bicycle assembly shop. It would work, but the profit margin was very low. Hence it required excellent management. Advice from my leaders was that, because of this, we were better to try another approach.

Many ideas were suggested and discussed and discussed...

Finally, vermiculture (the growing of worms) was decided upon. These would be exported to Japan, where they would be used for perfumes, for placing in wines to make 'macho' drink and for worm-burgers! The castings would make excellent potting soil for sale to rich people growing orchids. Jun started with a few kilos of worms and worked diligently at it. They doubled each month. After a year there was sufficient to begin selling. At about that time, the exporter quietly packed up his office and disappeared. Jun, exhausted by the work and expecting double the number of worms each month, had had enough. We are still seeking out alternatives. Where do you sell kilos of earthworms if not to Italians for perfume, Canadians for fish or Japanese for burgers?

Meanwhile discussions continue as to how to become a self-supporting pastor! Chicken runs are now being constructed...

A good man

There was a man in Tatalon, who had outdone many Christians in his service to the poor of the slums. He was a small worker clad in a pair of shorts and very intelligent. He owns a small joinery in Tatalon employing twenty workers. He buys cheap wood, builds cheap furniture, uses cheap transport (a horse and cart) and is kind to his workers. He has a degree in commerce.

The men working there are the local drinkers. He pays his twenty men relatively cheap wages, but he provides stable work and often provides piece-work for the children and the wives. It is better to have stable work than no work at all or insecure work. The men respect him. He sits with them and drinks with them. They say he knows *pakikisama* — how to get along with people, how to be one of the boys. That's a high compliment for a man.

This is the kind of industry the squatters need: a place where men can learn a skill while producing enough to run a business. Most unskilled men are unable to produce a first-class job at an economic price. This is not their fault, but their misfortune. Their unskilled life has never allowed them to become skilled craftsmen. Economic aid has to be focussed at the level of developing entrepreneurs who will lead others with them as they move up out of poverty.

One friend came to help with some electronics ideas. Another friend told of someone who was employing several squatter Christians in a shoemaking project. A welding shop seemed a feasible idea since there were many jeepney and tricycle body-building shops throughout Manila. Each one would require a person with management skills to develop and manage it. Over a period of time and the study of various economic projects develped by other groups, a conviction grew that with a team of three people with the right skills, a cottage industry/skills training project would succeed. For example, a woman trained in marketing, an engineer trained in production and someone with personnel/management skill would provide enough dynamic for most projects. Three people seemed a critical number in a consensus-oriented society.

It also was obvious that the West is full of down-to-earth, practical men who, with little equipment, can build most things they need and who have imbibed basic management skills from their culture. I began to pray for such men in their late thirties to forties: men with above-average sensitivity, men able to stick at such projects for sufficient time until the culture is mastered and the work established, men who can hold a hacksaw in one hand and a Bible in the other — who can, as they pass on skills, also pass on the love and power of the God at work within them. Grey-haired, retired executives would be a special gift from God. Families with children would have to live outside or on the edge of such squatter areas. However, in this particular role, a wise man could work from the outside.

Will renewal become revival?

Our minds are saturated with data contrasting rich nations with poor. We do not want to hear any more of the problem. Most Western Christians long to hear of potential *solutions* that they can be involved in.

The church in New Zealand has had a deep social conscience concerning the Third World poor. A significant percentage of non-Christians when asked, during the sixties and early seventies, to define what a Christian is would respond in terms of one who does good for his neighbour, gives to the poor, visits prisons and so on.

And partially they are right. For faith without practical evidence, according to both Jesus and James, is no faith at all. Evangelicals often define that evidence of faith as being baptism or a personal testimony (based on Romans 10:9, 10). These are evidences. Jesus, however, defines another evidence:

> Come . . . inherit the kingdom . . .
> For I was hungry and you gave me food,
> I was thirsty and you gave me a drink,
> I was a stranger and you welcomed me,
> I was naked and you clothed me,
> I was sick and you visited me,
> I was in prison and you came to me (Matthew 25:34-36).

While on furlough, I felt constrained to declare that unless the cleansing and renewal occurring in New Zealand churches resulted in a changed lifestyle — in economic repentance — they would never be consummated into true revival.

For affluence and worship do not result in pleasure to God.

A new spirituality must be outworked in new economics. Raised hands, ecstatic spiritual experiences and new worship forms in dance and music on their *own* are of no consequence to

God. They are not holy, but like a mud bath in his sight *unless* accompanied by economic repentance and justice. Listen to Isaiah:

> Bring no more vain offerings;
> Incense is an abomination to me.
> New moon and sabbath and the calling of assemblies –
> I cannot endure iniquity and solemn assembly
> (Isaiah 1:13).

Renewal has come. Social repentance had occurred along with and basic to renewal. The new love, ministry and spiritual experiences of thousands of house groups in every kind of New Zealand church has developed a distinctly effective Kiwi model of evangelism.

But just as in Acts the coming of the Holy Spirit was followed by economic repentance and new economic structures, so this must result in New Zealand. And this pattern has relevance throughout the Western world: in Australia, in the UK, in the USA.

Acts 2 and 4:

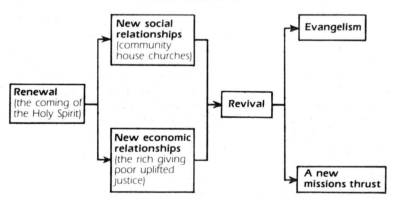

First, at a house group and church community level, there needs to be a commitment to economic sharing and, through this, to a simpler lifestyle. This will be the basis of a ministry of integrity to the poor.

Second, as a poor class emerges in the West as a result of the economic depression, the churches need to be ministering to them, drawing them into extended families and establishing work schemes.

Third, in relationship to the Third World, Western churches need to take leadership in national repentance for our continued exploitation of the Third World's resources, for our restrictive trade licensing system, our unjust balance of trade relationships with Third World nations and our totally inadequate aid policies. If the church does not repent, how can the government? The church is called to be the conscience of the nation.

Fourth, we need to get into the hands of the poor the means of production by:

(a) transferring our technical expertise through people who will give themselves long-term to learning another culture, identifying the level of local expertise and passing on appropriate technology.

(b) making available the equipment needed to assist Asia's urban poor to enter an industrial society at a small-scale industry level, either by donating it or by donating funds for it.

(c) getting funds to Asia's poor without interest and without unnecessary controls.

These constructive activities would all be components of economic repentance, a repentance from the sins of Sodom:

> Behold this was the guilt of your sister Sodom:
> she and her daughters had pride, surfeit of food
> and prosperous ease, but did not aid the poor and
> needy (Ezekiel 16:49).

Traditional Western churches have rejected these words from God. Those where a humbling before God and subsequent renewal have occurred have often heard these words gladly and taken action.

May I have your sewing machine?

There are many old ladies in the West who possess two sewing machines. We asked for them to give one. I did not dare suggest that their new one, used full-time in the hands of the poor lady, might be worth far more in heaven than the difficulties they themselves would have going back to their old one! With two exceptions, I received old ones. (So much for my lack of boldness!)

My own church is an unusual one. It has a number of wealthy executives, doctors and professionals who, nevertheless, have chosen simple homes and simple lifestyles and who delight in supporting missionaries. They had a 'Day of Jubilee' where many goods were brought for the poor as a sign of renewed commitment to simplicity. Nine crates of goods were marked for Manila.

Meanwhile, the team in Manila was planning what to do with the goods on arrival. Theresa and Resty were both engineers who came to be part of an economic projects committee. We discussed what we would do with the welding machine and the sewing machines. Could we set up a carpentry shop with the four carpenters who had been converted? Theresa prayed for a pair of glasses for Kid, who had frequently said he was unable to read the Bible because of poor eyesight.

The goods arrived. Four days of sweat, clearance through Customs (with no bribes!) and fifty-nine signatures later we were careering down the streets loaded to the nines. The Christians sorted and packed the clothing into plastic bags. Lo and behold, a pair of glasses! Only later did I discover that the church secretary had misplaced his glasses while packing the goods!

We went carolling, giving the clothes and shoes to the poorest widows and families. The first girl, a young woman who was now pregnant, began to weep. 'I thought I had no friends, nobody to love me,' she said.

The sewing machines were spirited away to Aling Berta's house. Gary and Berta had been two of the first to believe and were recognized as leaders within the community. Berta was the daughter of our *barrio* counsellor (equivalent to a town councillor). She immediately set in motion her plan to employ some women in turning off-cut cloth into rags that could be sold to jeepney drivers. Other machines are being used in dressmaking.

Importing company

To grapple with the issues related to unjust trade practices and to have a cottage industry outlet from Manila, I prayed for an evangelical importing company to be set up in New Zealand. (There is a large 'alternative' importing group in New Zealand that had begun from a Christian base but, as is so often the case in development work, has been influenced by Liberation theology. This makes association with it potentially dangerous in the politically volatile situation of the Philippines. Despite this problem, over the years this agency has effected a significant number of creative changes in New Zealand's trading policies.)

I prayed for a year. A week before returning to the field, a friend volunteered, in a casual conversation, with his house group to put up shares and set up such a company. Four cottage industries exist amongst the 14,000 residents of Tatalon: carpentry, cane chair-making, crochet and burricraft (a form of grass weaving). We spent many hours linking these up to another non-profit Christian exporting company. Existing Christian importers in New Zealand are excited about small non-profit ventures which can directly assist the poor within their existing frameworks. The involvement in importing is giving the house group a first-hand opportunity to apply the biblical teaching on helping the poor and on doing justice.

Prayer and economics

But taking on Satan in the area of economics, fighting the demon poverty, is not to be done without spiritual opposition. Behind these activities were long evenings of prayer. The Lord was evident during one particular evening in Tatalon. There were about twenty-five together that night. How beautiful it was to hear Aling Nena pray in Tagalog:

'Lord, help us; we're just poor people, but we know that before you there's neither rich nor poor. We're very poor, so help us. Please heal me from my sickness. I believe in you. I haven't been to the *albulario*! (spiritualist or faith healer).

'And Lord thank you for hearing me — for giving work to Eleanor, my daughter. And I want to thank Viv for giving her the capital!'

We had given Eleanor P200 (US$20) of the capital given to us for exporting goods so she could get started in running a meat stall in a market. She was repaying us P5 per day ($0.50), so we could recover the capital before the export goods left for New Zealand and use it for its designated purpose.

This project worked well. Others of the new believers asked if they, too, could take loans of P300 ($30), repaying them at a rate of P5 per day after the first two weeks, so that within three months they had repaid them. Helen was lent money for a dried fish stall; Liz and Rene for an eatery; another for *bagoong* (a tasty sauce made from ground anchovy fish). We talked together about improving the concept. An economic committee was set up. These were now their own projects — run with their own motivation. Control of the finances and economic development policy was now in their hands. The young fellowship was now establishing an economic identity reflecting principles of the kingdom!

And the future?

Dreams create work, so it is wisest not to have too many. With a goal of assisting every squatter Christian leader to gain a skill or become self-supporting, the dreams can be multiplied a hundredfold.

Soap-making, shoe manufacture, food stores and beekeeping (there are only about 400 beekeepers in the Philippines) have all been discussed. Microfarms that integrate ducks, fishponds, rice, goats, pigs, methane gas production and vegetables in a small area — and a multitude of other ideas — are all potential programs.

But each has a cost in time, money and management that has to be weighed and paid at the right season. Each has also to emerge from the felt needs and responses of the squatter Christians. Each has to be developed by someone trained to manage — and such personnel are hard to find amongst the poor.

William Booth summed up his experience in the area of economic programs amongst the converted poor:

> Most schemes that are put forward for the improvement of the people . . . would only affect the aristocracy of the miserable. It is the thrifty, the industrious, the sober, the thoughtful who can take advantage of these plans . . . No one will ever make a visible dent on the mass of squalor who does not deal with the improvident, the lazy, the vicious, the criminal. The scheme of social salvation is not worth discussing which is not as wide as the scheme of eternal salvation.

At the same time he outlined:

> I would not disguise the fact that I attach far more importance to reform of the man than to reform of the law. The problem of problems lies here in a nutshell . . .²

The missionary role

What is the role of the pioneer missionary in all of these things? Missionaries will never become one of the people. Always they will be guests in a culture despite mastery of language, cultural values and deep relationships.

The biblical word for missionary is apostle, or 'sent one'. Apostles are to pioneer, to reach into new areas, to establish new fellowships, laying the correct framework built on Jesus Christ. In this they must lead, set the pace, preach the word. Apostles are to direct the new believers to study of the scriptures for solutions to their own problems. In this they are to sit and listen, clarifying the issues, but letting the believers find their own solutions. The local Christians are the ones who understand the social structure, the economics and the politics of life around them. They are the ones who can bring socio-economic and political change within society. The missionary's role is to teach the breadth and depth of the scriptures, to provide the depth of theology needed for a movement.

Western missionaries of the late twentieth century must recognize at the same time that they are brothers and sisters to a clan and a nation of rich people. Behind them are great resources which, because of a commitment to justice and compassion, they must tap. And this requires management.

Jesus lived simply, but he, too, had behind him infinite resources. In one sense he was not poor, for his ministry sustained twelve men. He received money, but little of it stuck to his own hands.

The apostle is to initiate and yet seek to remain free from the administrative and managerial load that each economic and legal project demands. Free to pioneer new ideas, recruit new labourers, delegate tasks and set up the structures for them to function by. Free to continue preaching the word and opening up the next communities to the gospel. Free to live the carefree life so loved by a modern-day follower of Francis of Assissi.

The first apostles or church leaders were well aware of this problem. Initially they had to handle the economic interchange between rich and poor sparked off by the Holy Spirit but, as time went on, they realized the need to delegate the administration of a program for widows to seven deacons (for deacons read 'social workers', 'community developers' or 'administrators'):

> Therefore, brethren, pick out from among you seven men of good repute, full of the Spirit, and of wisdom whom we may appoint to this duty. But we will devote ourselves to prayer and the word (Acts 6:3-4).

They put priority on the spiritual dimensions.

Jesus did the same constantly. It has often worried me why Jesus, a carpenter, never set up a carpentry training program to help some of the poor. He cared enough for them. But he declared his vocation as being 'to preach the gospel to the poor. . .' and called the disciples to 'go, preach the gospel'.

Francis Schaeffer has described how theology has influenced philosophy, which then influences the arts and music and, from this, all areas of life.

Jesus knew that preaching the kingdom, confounding demonic powers and healing the sick was a priority. He was hitting at the canker in the core of society, not just the symptoms. At the same time he went about doing good.

It is at this point that Christian aid agencies become useful, with administrative structures already established to take Western money and give it to the poor.

A matter of perspective

The squatter views his slum as a piece of hope. The Western outsider views it as insanitary, full of disease, lacking in water, adequate housing, privacy, peace and quiet, trees and so on. It appears destitute in comparison with the neighbouring 'normal' middle-class subdivisions that can be observed elsewhere. These images for a Westerner are only a natural response were he to be suddenly thrown into a shanty town.

But for the slum dweller himself life is better than before. The standard of living in most slums is no lower than in the rural areas from which the inhabitants have recently come, nor is it, perhaps, very different from that of the industrial West a century ago. But it contrasts starkly with the technological affluence of the urban populations of the industrial nations and, even more pertinently, with that of the elite of the Third World.

The slum dweller finds cohesion and solidarity in these communities compared with the more affluent subdivisions. They provide opportunity for him to participate in a new technological world: in consumer goods, a better educational opportunity for his children and an increased average income over what he was able to earn in the province. The slums are 'bridgeheads' where, settled close to kin and to potential employment opportunities, he is able to seize upon the long-hoped-for opportunity. In such a context, the assistance of fellow Christians is viewed by all as a positive input to the community.

Often questions have been raised as to whether it is worth assisting these poor economically since, as they move up, they will move out of these areas. Apart from the obvious ethical fallacy in this statement, it is factually not true. Since about half of the areas identified by the government as squatter areas in Manila are to be upgraded, these have become stable places of residence. Numerous others are stable because of the lack of any need to shift them off an area of land.

Maslow's hierarchy of needs

Someone else may ask: If economic prosperity does not satisfy, why try and uplift these poor? The answer ultimately comes down to human dignity and the aim of disciplemaking — to bring people to the fulness of the character of Christ.

LEVELS OF NEED:

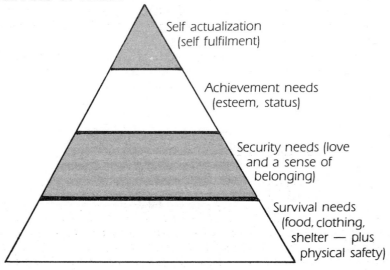

Self actualization (self fulfilment)

Achievement needs (esteem, status)

Security needs (love and a sense of belonging)

Survival needs (food, clothing, shelter — plus physical safety)

Abraham Maslow[3] points out that, until certain need levels are met, the next level of growth of a person cannot be expected.

When a person's basic food, clothing and housing needs are unmet, all attention is focussed on providing for these needs. For example, in the Nazi concentration camps there were no riots or sexual problems because all attention was on survival. People were treated in such situations as objects. Their worth was determined by their ability to contribute to survival.

If survival needs are met, but there are unresolved family tensions and insecurities, personal achievement will rarely occur. This is evidenced in slum families where bitterness and disorganized family structures result in an unwillingness to initiate or to carry through a job. Entrepreneurs may be found where both these levels of need are met and achievement needs become the motivational factor in life.

Those whose need levels are met at these three levels can work at the level of fulfilment and pure enjoyment. Such are the leisured classes. Out of these comes the dynamism that moulds culture.

The aim of disciple-making is developing men and women with the character of Christ and fulfilment at every level of need.

In a Third World country, you do not feed a man to convert him. But for him to reach full maturity of character, he must have food. Jesus knew this, so he was constantly meeting survival needs. As well, Jesus ministered to the security needs of his disciples by establishing a team, a social unit, and to their achievement needs by sending them out to minister. In such a context, he was able to bring them to fulfilment and personal wholeness.

This is what we call holistic discipling.

Footnotes on Chapter 10

1. Excerpts from Charles H. Troutman, 'A Fallacy in Church Planting: a Fable', *Evangelical Missions Quarterly*, July 1981, p 137
2. General Frederick Coutts, *Bread for My Neighbour*, Hodder and Stoughton, 1978
3. Maslow, A.H., *Motivation and Personality*, New York, Harper and Row, 1954

11

With Justice for All

SQUATTER POLITICS

THE WORKER IN THE SLUMS lives in a situation of oppression and exploitation. He must grapple with issues of injustice daily.

One day as I was walking down the road to my house the leader of the women's group called out her greetings. I went over and talked. She invited me in and began to tell me about an event some years ago.

The land-owner had many times ordered the squatters evicted. This time he brought both the court order and the local police chief. The squatters had had their warning! Behind him came a bulldozer to push down the squatter homes.

The protest began. The people, screaming, lay down and kneeled in front of it. The hired thugs of the land-owner dragged them away. The local priest arrived and calmed down the people. Talking to the bulldozer driver, he asked him to be patient. He was angry, too, but quietened down. Police reinforcements arrived. The priest organized people to lie down in front of the bulldozer. He kept talking of non-violence. He had talked with the police chief, mentioning that the mayor had been called and should be arriving soon...

What do you do when your people's homes are to be destroyed? What do you do in response to violence, murder, oppression and injustice? Does not your heart burn with anger and reaction, with the desire to fight back or to defend?

God feels the same way. He is a God of justice. He defends the poor and needy. In this case the mayor defended the squatters' rights. Years later, they obtained legal rights to the land.

Hungry for God

One day I stumbled across a small passage in Jeremiah 22:13-17. For years I had taught that the knowledge of God occurs through Bible reading and prayer. These activities are certainly basic to all else. But the logical outcome of such a doctrine was to spend more and more time in prayer and Bible reading and less and less in the activities of life. Ultimately one becomes a hermit.

This verse hit me: 'to know God' is 'to do justice and righteousness, to judge the cause of the poor and needy'.

A hunger for God throws us not into pietism, but into the thick of the injustices of this earth.[1]

'Justice and righteousness' is a phrase similar to our concept of social justice.[2] Perhaps, since the phrase 'social justice' has left-wing or activist overtones, we might say it is similar to living 'just lifestyles' — in whatever work or area of social responsibility we live in, to bring just dealings, create just programs, reform unjust practices or stand against unjust actions.

The missionary call

God is a God of justice. From these devastated masses of destitute humanity that are Manila's slums, three million cries for help and mercy reverberate around the throne room and entry halls of his court.

God hears! And he rises in indignation and anger!

And he looks for one who will stand before him for the poor of this city. Two thousand years ago, finding none, he sent his own Son, declaring:

> Behold, my servant whom I uphold,
> My chosen one in whom my soul delights.
> I have put my spirit upon him;
> He will bring forth justice to the nations (Isaiah 42:1).

Notice his choosing. Note his empowering. And note his purpose: a missionary call to bring forth justice to the ends of the earth. It is these same thoughts that Jesus repeats in Luke 4:18, when he said the Spirit of the Lord was upon him to preach the gospel to the poor. Jesus' gospel was good news to the oppressed, good news of a kingdom where justice will be done.

Note also the servant's methodology, his manner of bringing justice:

> He will not cry or lift up his voice,
> or make it heard in the street . . . (verse 2)

This is no high-flying diplomat on shuttle diplomacy. Nor is he an articulate demonstrator, loud-hailer in hand. Nor yet is he a flashy, travelling evangelist with glossy promotional materials.

> No rich King this, with heralds before him!
> But gentle. For this King comes as a servant,
> softly;
> this kingdom breaks iron bars
> and sets prisoners free.
> It storms the gates of hell,
> but quietly, graciously, gently.

He comes humbly, riding on an ass, washing others' feet, putting back sword-cut ears. Isaiah tells of the Messiah's gentleness:

> a bruised reed he will not break
> and a dimly burning wick
> he will not quench . . . (verse 3)

He gently binds up those of us who are broken reeds. He doesn't snap us off. And those who are almost to be burned out he does not snuff out like a candle wick between his fingers. Instead, he fans us back until we become a blazing light.

Such is God's method of bringing justice. And this justice is sure:

> He will not fail or be discouraged till he has established justice
> in the earth . . . (verse 4)

And we are his body, called to the same role as our Master. We are servants of the Servant. For 'if anyone serve me, he must follow me; and where I am there shall my servant be also'. How high a calling!

Paul takes on this role, claiming as the basis of his lifestyle a passage from another one of these servant songs. It defined the task of the servant as follows:

> My servant . . . I will give you as a light to the nations that my
> salvation may reach to the end of the earth (Isaiah 49:6).

We, too, are called to declare this salvation to the ends of the earth — as God's servants. Incarnating God is to incarnate justice and righteousness in a servant lifestyle:

For he delivers the needy when he calls,
the poor and him who has no helper
He has pity on the weak and needy
and saves the lives of the needy
From oppression and violence he redeems their life
and precious is their blood in his sight
(Psalm 72:12-14).

Personal justice

There are four levels of doing justice: first, in personal dealings; second, in peacemaking, bringing reconciliation between parties; third, the establishing of movements who live justly; fourth, effecting changes at the upper levels of society.

The first level of justice begins in the fear of the Lord. For the oppressed have a weapon. When they cry to the Lord, the Lord hears them and acts on their behalf. This gives one a deep fear of causing offence or humiliating a poor man.

Such justice begins in small things. One time I forgot to pay the girl from the squatter home next door. She typed for me two or three days weekly. I was travelling, almost to my destination at a conference in the province, when I got that sinking feeling in my stomach: 'Oh no, I forgot to pay my typist'. Into my mind flashed the verse:

You shall not oppress a hired servant who is poor and needy. . .
You shall give him his hire on the day he earns it, before the sun
goes down (for he is poor, and sets his heart upon it); lest he
cry against you to the Lord and it be sin in you (Deuteronomy
24:14-15).

But personal uprightness in its biblical context includes social justice as well as justice in small things. Ezekiel describes righteousness in this way, describing the righteous person as one who:

. . .does not oppress any one, but restores to the debtor his
pledge, commits no robbery, gives his bread to the hungry and
covers the naked with a garment, does not lend at interest or

take any increase, withholds his hand from iniquity, executes true justice between man and man, walks in my statutes and is careful to observe my ordinances — he is righteous (Exekiel 18:7).

The end of the road

But being a rich man amongst the poor requires more than personal justice with a social component. In a situation of injustice and oppression, discipleship involves a second level of doing justice: peacemaking, bringing reconciliation between parties, seeking justice for those unjustly treated.

'Open your mouth, judge righteously, maintain the rights of the poor and needy,' commands the King of Massa in Proverbs 31. And that is dangerous. The disciple in the slums will alternately be labelled CIA or Marxist, depending on who is exercising bitterness against him. Neither label is correct, for we work neither for the communist nor capitalist cause. We work only to do the righteousness of the kingdom.

Consider the sad letter from my *kumadre*, my 'blood sister':

Eli has now no employer, so we are not earning even a single penny. We are just making a living through borrowing and debts. With regard to our kids, they are often contaminated by common illnesses successively. You know, Viv, we do not know how to solve our problems. Incidentally, the government agency that owns our land is asking us to vacate the place where we are in for the reason of not remitting our payment since we have lived here . . .

The response was to help with payment. The next letter was worse, explaining how the cost of P3,825 for their house had now become P9,460 over two-and-a-half years.

Doing justice means finding out whether this 300% increase in a house price is due to unjust policies written by the government authority or whether a corrupt official is the cause. It means rectifying the situation. It means giving to my brother and sister in need, never expecting it back. It means finding work for my *kumpadre*. And where my lack of resources and time make all of this impossible immediately, it means looking to God to bring his judgement on the men who perpetuate such legal crimes. For God:

> . . .will not revoke the punishment
> because they sell the righteous for silver,
> and the needy for a pair of shoes —
> they that trample the head of the poor into the dust
> of the earth, and turn aside the way of the afflicted. . .
> (Amos 2:6-7).

A God for the poor

Poverty is not caused only by the personal sins of the poor. The lack of absolute truth or ethics that is inherent in an animistic culture, plus centuries of injustice, exploitation and oppression by the provinces' leading families, by Spanish priests, by American businessmen and by the Japanese war machine have all contributed to this family's poverty in a highly productive province. Feudal barons who own the land farmed by tenants reinvest their profits in industry, land speculation and multinational companies in Manila. Eventually the money is shipped out of the economy through the multinationals to the United States, Japan and elsewhere. Castillo in his book *Beyond Manila* [3] provides a well-researched analysis of the structural causes and effects of Philippine rural poverty — a major cause of urban poverty.

The injustice cries out from the land!

One day I was out jogging in the country (sometimes one does culturally unacceptable things like jogging on one's own). I wiped some sweat from my eyes, stopped and looked past the guard through the massive gates of a mansion. It cost two million pesos I had been told.

I jogged on to the basketball court and asked by new-found farming friends where the money came from to build it. They sat around on their haunches, joking back and forth about the question. In between the jokes (a way of covering embarrassment or shame) they told me how most of the local families gave fifty per cent of their crop to this landlord. Before the land reform law was implemented, he used to provide them with help if they were sick or in need. Those that had obtained ownership rights to the land no longer received such help; they just went into debt to the money-lender. The money-lender charged a much higher rate than the landlord exacted (for every five pesos, the lender receives six pesos the next day — this system is called 'five-six').

Proverbs comments: 'The fallow ground of the poor yields much food, but it is swept away by injustice' (13:23). Isaiah describes how 'The wicked trample the oppressed poor underfoot' (26:6).

There are few of the rural poor who are not constantly confronted with these injustices. A government job is not much better.

Susan moved into an accountant's position in the local municipal office. They 'fiddle' the books for profit. The auditor is in the know. He receives his cut. The investigator from the Bureau of Internal Revenue is paid off when he comes.

How can Susan work as an auditor and survive as a Christian? If she exposes the system or rebels against it she will lose her job. It is a difficult problem.

As I studied and reflected on their poverty, I read that it is these poor that God defends and protects (Proverbs 29:7 and 3l:9). Some intimate that God has a class consciousness and is involved in a class war. This is a slight exaggeration. The scriptures do not follow a Marxist analysis of class war. God does appear to have a bias for the poor, standing against the rich (James 5:1-6), but it is only an *apparent* bias, a bias only in comparison with our own lack of concern. He is a just God, a compassionate God, but also an impartial God.

As a good father will protect his youngest from being beaten by his eldest son *precisely because* he is good and just, so God particularly prefers, protects and identifies with the poor. But let us not call him partial. He treats *all* as of infinite value and worth. Thus he involves himself with the less fortunate, condemning our unconcerned luxurious living as well as our oppression, as James says:

Come now, you rich, weep and howl for the miseries that are coming upon you. Your riches have rotted and your garments are moth-eaten. Your gold and silver have rusted, and their rust will be evidence against you and will eat your flesh like fire. You have laid up treasure for the last days. Behold the wages of the labourers who mowed your fields, which you kept back by fraud, cry out; and the cries of the harvesters have reached the ears of the Lord of hosts. You have lived on the earth in luxury and in pleasure; you have fattened your hearts in a day of slaughter. You have condemned, you have killed the righteous man, he does not resist you. (5:1-6).

Community development

This leads to the third level of doing justice in the slums. This is to establish movements of believers who:

(a) demonstrate justice in their lifestyles with each other
(b) begin to bring justice into the life and leadership of their immediate community.

Again it began in small things, such as that evening when he filled me with a desire to pray about the rubbish!

Doing justice begins in prayer. Biblical politics means calling on a higher authority. Rubbish is a little issue, but it is involvement with God in little issues that affects the community. This gives the Christian leader the freedom and respect to relate to community leaders and officials on more major issues such as when the land owner brought in bulldozers to push down the people's homes. I thought a lot about what I would have done if I had been the spiritual leader of the community at that time. It seemed important that my immediate responsibility was to become a recognized spiritual leader within the community, with sufficient depth of relationship to be called for advice should the same situation be repeated.

Just lifestyles must be seen in believers first. The church must be established in justice, as a reference point for non-believers.

John Perkins has described the growth of a community of believers who demonstrate justice in their relationships in a racially torn community. His dream was 'to carve out of the heart of Jackson, Mississippi, a community of believers reconciled to God and to each other. To bring together a fellowship of blacks and whites, rich and poor. Such could make a positive difference in the lives of a community enslaved by poverty and racism.'4

Some view planting the church as establishing a small group of believers who live in the kingdom of God *within* the community. Others view it as more than this — as establishing the kingdom of God *over* the slum community. Growing up within an Anabaptist and fundamentalist heritage meant my first years of church planting were focussed on a separated group of believers *within* a community.

Such separated communities have, paradoxically, brought many major political changes into our own society, acting as true lights, bright beacons on a hill. Because of their strong concept of rescuing people from damnation, they have often become deeply involved in the problems of their age. Thus Quakers developed the early mental hospitals; the Salvation Army the first sheltered workshop schemes; the Mennonites have consistently worked at peacemaking nationally and internationally. Today often non-religious social work is a verson of activities developed by such groups. Early Anabaptists enunciated separation of church and state, religious liberty and the role of free choice in matters of faith, each of which became major political issues in their time.[5]

But the urgent cries of the poor, the study of Booth, of Kagawa, of Calvin and of Wesley and their work amongst the poor, as well as the history of missions, kept forcing me back to the scriptures.

Passages such as Proverbs 11:10 11,'When it goes well with the righteous, the city rejoices. . . By the blessing of the upright a city is exalted', indicate an active involvement by the righteous in community leadership and lead one to a desire to establish the kingdom within every level of society — and, where the social structure permits (as in Calvin's Geneva or Tonga last century),[6] over society.

There is a principle portrayed in Jeremiah's prophecy to the exiled Israelites when they were taken to Babylon:

> Build houses and live in them;
> plant gardens and eat their produce.
> Take wives and have sons and daughters. . .
> But **seek the welfare of the city** where I have sent you
> into exile, and pray to the Lord on its behalf, for in
> its welfare you will find your welfare (Jeremiah 29:7).

As aliens and exiles, always looking towards our heavenly home, we too are wise to seek the welfare of the cities in which we are living. Because our future in the kingdom is secure, we should not sit back and do nothing. Rather all the more we should seek to bring the principles of that kingdom to bear on the structures of society in which we find ourselves. This is love for our neighbour. This is being ambassadors of our King and this is the basis of Christian community development.

Upper-class evangelism

The fourth level of doing justice is to effect changes at the upper levels of society. Over the years I've found many who are developing theologies of justice who speak proudly of working at this level. But few of us in fact are called to do so.

For most of us, God has called us to do our apprenticeship: to start where we are with what we've got and do what we can at a community level. This may be first in establishing communities of believers, alternative economic structures and small businesses, then in motivating local politicians to do right and confronting local leaders with their wrongs. God may then give grace for a wider field of ministry, but let us not be arrogant.

On the other hand it is those Christians of the upper-class, committed in bringing the kingdom of God *into* or *over* every aspect of society, who have most affected social change within society. For the rich are the key to the poverty of the poor.

The process of social breakdown

I went back to the Bible to study justice. What causes a society to become unjust? The steps are outlined clearly in Isaiah 59:12-16:

> We know our iniquities...
> speaking oppression and revolt...
> Justice is turned back...
> for truth has fallen in the public squares
> and uprightness cannot enter...
> The Lord saw it and it displeased him that
> there was no justice;
> He saw that there was no man,
> and wondered that there was no one to intervene
> (no intercessor).
> Then his own arm brought him victory,
> and his righteousness upheld him.

First 'our transgressions are multiplied before thee' — little sins, little deviations. This results in the second step of 'transgressing, denying the Lord and turning away from following our God'. Then comes the bitterness of the revolutionary, the Marxist, the liberation theologian on the one hand 'speaking revolt', and the capitalist exploiter, the corrupt bureaucrat and the self-serving politician on the other 'speaking oppression'. (Note how oppression goes with revolution.)

To justify terrorism and revolt on the one hand or to justify more oppressive 'law and order' (that is law and order beyond ethics) on the other, people then begin 'conceiving and uttering from the heart lying words'.

'Justice is turned back, and righteousness stands afar off.' Note how justice and righteousness go together. Marxists link justice with revolt. God does not. Right-wing leaders link justice to oppression (law and order). God does not. He links it to truth:

> For truth has fallen in the public squares, and uprightness cannot enter. Truth is lacking, and he who departs from evil makes himself a prey.

What then is the biblical solution?

> The Lord saw it and it displeased him that there was no justice. He saw that there was no man, and wondered that there was no-one to intervene . . .

His method is available people of righteousness, those who understand true justice and are willing to intervene. Dare we be those people? Does he find such who will dare to intervene in the slums today? But failing to find such people, then God himself intervenes: 'his own arm brought him victory'.

The most famous group of upper-class Christians in our own English history were the Clapham Sect, friends of Wilberforce, a group of influential noblemen, bankers, politicians and industrialists in the late eighteenth and early nineteenth century.[7] At one time they infiltrated and took over the entire directorate of the East India Company, using it to champion the rights of the native races! Their persistent advocacy of morality in all dealings with subject nations did much to create notions of trusteeship and responsible imperial government. The relief of debtors, the destruction of slavery, the mitigation of the savage eighteenth century penal code, the ending of discrimination against Jews, Catholics and Protestant dissenters, the provision of charity to the victims of the Industrial Revolution — these reforms and others like them were effected by these evangelists.

Today, God continues to look for leaders of such truth and justice.

Effective social change
Why then work with the poor of the slums, when the great societal changes needed to assist the poor are affected by the rich and cannot be effected by working with the poor?

First, mass movements eventually produce changes in those at the top of society. The members of the Clapham Sect were the direct descendents of the Wesleyan revival. McLelland in a significant study on the psychological and social environment needed to create *entrepreneurs* (people who pioneer new businesses, the key to economic productivity) shows that the two great waves of achievement in England (fifty years after Wesley and the late nineteenth century) were each associated with Protestant reform or revival. The strong concern for Christian perfection in this world tended to produce an achievement orientation in Methodist sons, which turned the boys to business. Fifty years after the revival, the country reached a peak of achievement as these men entered national and business leadership![8]

Perhaps our primary political activity, then, is to establish movements of men and women converted and passionately committed to holiness. Acting like leaven in bread, such movements ultimately will transform society.

Second, upper-class politics is a question of power. The assumption that the centre of power is the Prime Minister or the President is based on a non-Christian concept of power.

Establishing 'power bases' amongst the poor may be the key. By this I mean bases of *spiritual* power — not Marxist or political power, but bases of people able to influence the One who rules over politicians, and hence able to obtain what they need by a non-political concept of power. This may, perhaps, be a more effective emphasis.

Such power to move the hand that moves the world can be utilised by poor Christians well taught in the scriptural injunction:

I urge that supplications, prayers, intercessions and thanksgivings be made for all men, for kings and all who are in high positions, that we may lead a quiet and peaceable life, godly and respectful in every way (1 Timothy 2:1-2).

Such prayers are not the intoned set phrases at weekly worship in dead churches. They are the prayers of people who know how to prevail on God to implement political change, who recognize that 'The King's heart is a stream of water in the hand of the Lord; he turns it wherever he will' (Proverbs 21:1).[9]

Righteous poor people who possess spiritual power while renouncing natural concepts of power, people who know the issues of the time, poor wise men and women — these are, perhaps, the key to social change. Such learned people, unable to be bought by wealth or power, are the key to godly societies.

St Francis Xavier, the nobleman who renounced social status and opened up Asia for the gospel, was such a poor wise man. He won to Christ tens of thousands in India, the Moluccas and Japan. He did it by means of washing the wounds of lepers, praying for the healing of the sick and preaching the gospel. He sagely commented: 'The world is not ruled by principles of politics or economics, but by the mysterious realities of sin and grace'.[10]

Third, one works with the poor rather than the rich because of the example of Jesus. He could have come as a rich man, come as the great welfare king. Instead he came as a babe in a Bethlehem manger, surrounded by shepherds. He had a reason, though we understand it poorly, for identification with and ministry amongst the poor. He had a reason for refusing Herod's courts and Satan's offer.

Doing justice for Jesus involved riding not on a centurion tank, but on an ass. His heroes were children and slaves, not generals and politicians. At the time when he could have overthrown the unjust Romans and their empire (72,000 angels are a match for most Roman legions), he was putting back an ear.

But there will come a day when he will return with sword in hand, when the grapes of wrath will be pressed out and judgement on oppression, evil and sin will be executed:

He will not fail or be discouraged
till he has established justice on the earth . . . (Isaiah 42:4).

Jesus set us a model as a revolutionary who never revolted, as a man of power who refused others' concepts of power, a man of justice who refused to be others' judge, as a man with his spirit attuned to the heavens who was constantly involved in dust and dirt, pain and people.[11]

Part of Jesus' genius in working with the poor was that the rich came to him as well. Nicodemus searched out Jesus, because of Jesus' credentials. It was not Jesus' political power that attracted him. It was his observation of Jesus' spiritual power worked out in signs amongst the poor. 'Rabbi,' he said, 'we know that you are a teacher come from God; for no one can do these signs that you do unless God is with him' (John 3:2).

In the same way living amongst the poor of Manila gives

credibility and an opening to the upper-class, for many upper-class Filipinos have a highly developed social conscience and are actively involved in helping the poor of their country.

Rothie was such a man: a politician, an academic, a former revolutionary, a man of integrity and compassion. During the Indonesian communist uprising, Rothie and a friend had flown to Indonesia to fight for justice. Later as the executive assistant of a university he had worked to clean up its corruption. This resulted in 117 staff being fired by presidential order — only to be reinstated when Libya put 'oil' pressure on those in political power! Rothie left quickly.

For a year he was afraid to leave his house, but began to work with the local fishermen, seeking to break the cycle of poverty in which they lived. First he provided a punt boat which enabled their canoes to travel further out to sea, reap bigger catches and extend their fishing season because of greater safety during the monsoon. He then looked into the marketing of the fish. He established a cool store, so the fish could be sold when the price was highest. Next he helped the fishermen's wives to become productive with gardening, goats and sewing.

I met him after he had come to a personal knowledge of Jesus Christ. From the moment I met Rothie I loved him, for he was a man who sought after justice with all his heart.

Once he told of the time when he was an executive in the university. There were visiting Arab dignitaries, so a great feast was organized. Rothie made sure all was in order and all felt adequately feted, then he and his wife quietly stepped out the back door to their own room and ate canned sardines and rice. Here was a man committed to justice, not only in society, but also in his own lifestyle.

One week he flew home from meeting with government leaders where he was seeking rights for a minority group he was assisting. He told me, 'I have cleared my desk. I have three days. I want you to teach me the scriptures!' Now this is a deeply humbling experience for a young, insecure, poorly-taught missionary. My mind raced. What do you teach a brilliant anthropologist-politician? Into my mind flashed the contrast between God's political perspective and society's.

'We will work through the book of Daniel. I think it will help you see God's ways of effecting political change.' The only basis of rapport I could have with such a man was that I cared enough about his people, the poor, to live with them.

The loyal reformers

The Lord gave entrance to other upper-class Christians in Manila who are working to bring justice for the poor within the structures of the government. These men speak prophetically to the government and speak out against sin at all levels in society — personally and politically, from a position of due respect and honour for those in power. And this is what the Bible teaches. We are to 'pay respect to whom respect is due, honour to whom honour is due' (Romans 13:7), to 'honour all men, love the brotherhood, fear God and honour the emperor' (1 Peter 2:17) — even if he has no clothes!

These passages were written in the context of the great exploitation, oppression and Machiavellian politics of the Roman empire, so they are independent of the evils of the man at the top.

A typical example of a man with an entree to the seat of power was a colonel, an advisor to the President, whose task was to prepare plans for a sugar factory complex. Having just been converted, he consumed book after book on the Christian basis for socio-political and economic development. He thought through a Christian framework as a basis for management-labour relations and profit sharing. His proposals were the basis for discussions at the highest level of government, discussions that inevitably meant discussing aspects of the gospel.

For basic to labour relations are a whole host of biblical concepts on work, justice and love. Take just one statement to employers:

> You shall not oppress a hired servant who is poor and needy, whether he is one of your brethren, or one of the sojourners who is in your land, within your towns (Deuteronomy 24:14).

This brief statement would radically reform a large percentage of the factories and close some multinationals in Manila if it were applied in practice!

The Bible is a never-to-be-put-down textbook on such issues as labour, profit making, work, successful management patterns and many other areas of business and politics. For people in high positions, the Bible clearly points out the responsibilities towards the poor.

A liberation theologian, in an excellent summary of the biblical perspective, comments:

The Bible speaks of positive and concrete measures to prevent poverty from becoming established among the people of God. In Leviticus and Deuteronomy, there is very detailed legislation designed to prevent the accumulation of wealth and the consequent exploitation. It is said, for example, that what remains in the fields after the harvest and the gathering of olives and grapes should not be collected; it is for the alien, the orphan, the widow (Deut. 24:19-21; Lev. 19:9, 10). Even more, the fields should not be harvested to the very edge so that something remains for the poor and the aliens (Lev. 23:22). The Sabbath, the day of the Lord, has a social significance; it is a day of rest for the slave and the alien (Ex. 23:12; Deut. 5:14). The triennial tithe is not to be carried to the temple; rather it is for the alien, the orphan and the widow (Deut. 14:28, 29; 26:12). Interest on loans is forbidden (Ex. 22:25; Lev. 25:35-37; Deut. 23:20). Other important measures include the Sabbath year and the jubilee year. Every seven years, the fields will be left to lie fallow 'to provide food for the poor of your people' (Ex. 23:11; Lev. 25:2-7), although it is recognized that this duty is not always fulfilled (Lev. 26:34, 35). After seven years, the slaves were to regain their freedom (Ex. 21:2-6), and debts were to be pardoned (Deut. 15:1-18). This is also the meaning of the jubilee year of Lev. 25:10 ff. It was . . . a general emancipation . . . of all the inhabitants of the land. The fields lay fallow; every man re-entered his ancestral property, i.e. the fields and houses which had been alienated returned to their original owners.[12]

But it is difficult to function at upper levels of leadership within a corrupt society. The higher up the ladder, the greater the extent of corruption. It is not unusual under an oppressive regime for a Christian to reach a high level in government and business, only to have to resign on an issue of injustice.

The more corrupt a society's leaders become, the less Christians are free to function. The church then moves more and more into an Anabaptist, separatist lifestyle. Theologies based on those of Calvin and Luther become less effective. For they grew their theologies in particular contexts where Christians had freedom to play a role at the upper levels of society.

It is interesting to see this principle work out in the roles of the prophets. The pre-exilic prophets in the Old Testament (Amos, Hosea, Micah, Isaiah and Jeremiah) worked from outside of the establishment, perhaps because of the extent of its evil, whereas the post-exilic prophets (Joel, Haggai, Zechariah and Malachi) worked from within the established political and religious leadership. The situation facing emerging Christian leadership in developing countries today is more akin to the pre-exilic one.

Demonic politics

There are many like the pre-exilic prophets who, whilst 'respecting the Emperor', stand in political opposition.

Amongst them, many upper-class Christians often recognise not only the political issues, but also the spiritual powers that function behind governments. Daniel understood such issues. At one stage it took one of the chief angels three weeks to break out of a battle with the 'prince of the kingdom of Persia' and reach Daniel. This supernatural being had delayed him until finally Gabriel had come to relieve him (Daniel 10:13).

It is against such 'principalities and powers, against the world rules of this present darkness, against the spiritual hosts of wickedness in the heavenly places' that we are to wrestle when entering the realm of the political. That is why prayer is our most potent political weapon.

Most politicians are men of the world, men who live outside of the word of God. But there are men in power who have been overtaken not only by sin, but also by these demonic principalities and powers. We readily recognize this in Hitler (even a cursory reading of his life shows all the classic symptoms of demonic possession), in Idi Amin or Colonel Gadaffi. The structures that such men create are not only corrupted by the world, as are all structures to come degree, but may be demonized — as with Naziism, Marxism and Capitalism. Colossians chapter 2 tells us that there are human philosophies and religious traditions that are perpetrated by the elemental spirits of the universe. It goes on to tell us that such 'principalities and powers' are disarmed (rendered inoperative) by the cross.[13]

In reading hundreds of articles on community and national development I saw that, ultimately, all non-Christian philosophies are darkened. Sometimes an article will glean some elements of truth. One gets excited waiting for the writer to come to the biblical conclusion, only to watch him or her miss the essential insight and fall back into darkness and the vagueness of relativity.

Marx and Marxism have obvious demonic influences. This is evident whenever relating to Marxist social workers: the bitterness effuses out of them. The desire to create bitterness that marked Marx as a man and was evidenced in his family relationships appears to result in distrust and violence wherever Marxism gains a hold.

This is evident, too, in the attempted Marxist takeover of the World Council of Churches and in the destructive influence of much German liberal theology on personal faith and piety. The early loss of a commitment to supernatural revelation ('demythologizing' the scriptures) has meant the historical Jesus Christ, the resurrection and the second coming are now relegated to myths. The aim of mission has become socio-political action seeking to bring 'shalom' to the world — this being interpreted as the harmony and unity of the world, the time when mankind brings in the kingdom of God. Evangelism is supposed to destroy such unity, so the concept is reinterpreted as being 'conscientization' through 'solidarity' with the poor (living with, identifying with the poor), bringing the masses to understand their plight in order to rise up and rectify it. If this sounds strongly influenced by Marxism, it is. This became evident in discussions about the youth work of one of the older denominations in the Philippines, deeply influenced by such thinking. Their youth program has been entirely restructured into activist cells!

Having turned Christ into a myth by demythologizing him, there is little direction for a church except political activism. The loss of ethics that results from the loss of authority of the scriptures eventually brings bitterness and lawlessness. Fighting for justice without the power of God and the ability to rely on him results in facing the impossible with our own inadequacy.[14]

Typical of this burnt-out hostility was my experience with the head of a national aid agency. I had gone to discuss some possibilities of co-operating together in some economic projects. We talked at length of the many complex issues. While speaking of justice for the poor, cigarette smoke rolled and drifted across the room, swearing made the air heavy with hate and the bitterness pouring out of his heart told me that this man was no servant of Christ's, even though he owned that name. His commitment to social justice was not matched by a commitment to personal holiness. This can never be! A bad tree cannot bear good fruit. Jesus tells us 'by the fruit of their lips you shall know them'. A lack of a daily intake of the word of God leads to a lack of personal ethics and ultimately to a twisted social ethic.

Similarly within the Catholic Church, liberation theology,

while rejected by the church itself, has been a vehicle for the bitter demon of Marxism to take a strong hold over many priests and nuns. One day I visited the bearded priest who had lived in Tatalon before me — a good man who had worked hard. Yet it was sad to see this well-meaning priest, with a deep love for the poor, burned up with bitterness. In trying to do good, his own innate evil had overtaken and was destroying him.

Sadly, this is the plight of many unregenerate social workers amongst the poor. Without workable solutions and without recourse to God as an effective higher authority, there can be no rest for their souls, no joy in their service and no tangible hope in their programs. Colossians chapter 2 talks not only of philosophies such as Marxism or Capitalism (with its deliberate base of greed)[15] being demonic; it tells us that empty religious traditions are also controlled by principalities and powers.

So, as a worker in the slums seeking to bring justice, one is in direct confrontation with powerful demonic forces. One stands, on the one hand against American capitalism in its form of exploitation by multinationals; on the other against Marxism, espoused by concerned priests and social workers; and yet again, against the older empty religious traditions of an unregenerate Catholicism and the deceitful 'double-talk' of the 'liberal' but politically active Protestant groups.

How do we confront such demons? By love and reconciliation with people. While rejecting the demonic philosophies, we honour and respect all men, recognizing the godliness of most Catholic priests, the genuine searchings of the Marxist social worker, or the good intentions of the 'liberal' pastor.

John Perkins sums up his own experience in a paragraph which, in many ways, is the crux of his book, *With Justice for All*:

Demanding our rights had not softened the white community as we hoped it would. Instead it had stiffened their opposition. Lying there on my bed I was able to see that confronting white people with hostility was only going to create war. If there was going to be any healing, it would have to **take place in an atmosphere of love**. I had been trying to **demand justice**. Now God was opening my eyes to a new and better strategy — seeking reconciliation. I could not bring justice for other people. As a Christian, my responsibility was to seek to be reconciled. Then out of reconciliation justice would flow.

> Affirmative action, integration and so on might be useful, but
> they alone were not justice . . . True justice could come only as
> people's hearts were made right with God and God's love
> motivated them to be reconciled to each other.[16]

Contention with authorities

Truthfulness, definding the right and contending for truth are
forms of doing right. Jesus was no spineless coward. When
slapped on the face and treated unjustly, he demanded, 'Why do
you strike me?' When faced with the Pharisees utilizing their
authority wrongly, an authority given by men but not by God, he
refused to recognise it. 'You brood of vipers,' is not a statement of
a politician trying to win votes by compromise. He was
establishing a kingdom and he was its rightful King.

Nor were the Old Testament prophets weak in their opposition
to evil. At the same time in dealing with authorities, it is evident
time and time again that God's spokemen in the scriptures
recognized that he had appointed such human authorities. Whilst
speaking forcefully to their sins, there is never a call to those under
authority to rise up in rebellion,[17] though there is a cry to defend
one's cultural identity, and frequently a call to those in authority
to repent and do right.

Moses, whilst leading an oppressed minority out from
oppression, went to the Pharoahs to gain permission, ultimately
leaving it to God's wrath to gain his end. David, whilst outlawed
from his society, refused to fight his king, leaving it to God to
judge his case. Jude tells us that when the archangel Michael was
contending with the devil about the body of Moses, he did not
presume to pronounce a reviling judgement, but said, 'The Lord
rebuke you.'

But, we need beware at the same time of teaching submission,
gentleness and obedience to authority as implying humble
acquiescence to unjust structures and unjust men in authority.
'Honour to those whom honour is due' and a loving and
reconciling spirit is not in conflict with contending for truth or
standing for the rights of the poor. Rather, it defines the context
and attitudes behind contention.

We must, if we are grounded in the scriptures, reject the idea
that if evil controls some government leaders, our response should
be to raise a revolution. That would be to fight evil with evil,
demon with demon.

Ezekiel 45:9 has two interesting couplets: 'Put away *violence and oppression* and execute *justice and righteousness*. Violence and oppression are linked together. They are the opposite of social justice. As oppression (sometimes called 'the first violence' by liberationalists) occurs, so rebellion and violence flare — and eventually revolution. Marxists encourage violent revolution as a way of overcoming oppression. Here the Bible plainly labels both extremes as the opposite of social justice. Righteousness and justice, not violence and bitterness, are the vanquishers of oppression.

Time and change

The crux of our rejection of revolutionary violence is the biblical concept of time and change.

Marxism presupposes that gradual reforms of society are too slow, that the political structures are too evil. Therefore, by escalating the bitterness and bloodletting, the evil will be destroyed by *sudden change*. What incredible logic!

Reformers within capitalist societies conceive of *managed change*, recognizing that violent change unleashes forces into a community that destroy its fabric for generations.[18]

Christians recognize both components of change. Their action is to preach repentance — introducing reform step-by-stop into a society, keeping it from going rotten. But a repentance too that recognizes that some societies and structures within society (take for instance white slavery) are so evil that God will violently destroy them not by our increasing violence, but by leaders who bring national repentance and transformation. Failing to find such people, God intervenes by his own arm.

Such was the case of Nineveh in Jonah's day. Because the world's greatest city of its time repented, God did not destroy it!

Gradual reforms and revolutions will all work towards bringing a one world government. But we are not optimistic that a one world government will be good and create 'shalom'. Christian reforms keep society from rottenness, but we must recognize our inability to make it holy.

We may agree with the Marxist analysis that the increasing centralization of power in the hands of rich capitalists plus the UN, the IMF, the EEC and related structures is enabling the rich industrial nations to increasingly exploit the poorer nations, and that this world economic system needs to be replaced with one based on equity and justice. But we also proclaim that our only hope of destroying this current unjust system is the return of the Just One.

God is not slow concerning his promises to return, but at the same time is patient, not willing that any should perish. He delays justice to salvage many, just as he waited 400 years before sending Jonah to Nineveh.

Sometimes, as I look at the great millions of poor through Manila, I wonder how long God can bear such a situation to continue. How his heart must weep and his anger blaze, yet he waits to be merciful.

And he will delay this final revolution, brought by his own arm and those of the heavenly host. He will delay it till the one world government has become so great in its exploitation and is under so total a control of one world ruler, that humankind has no more hope and the time for repentance has gone.

Reforms are not reform enough. Revolutions are not revolutionary enough. But God's strategy is a long-term strategy that cannot fail. His kingdom, like a grain of mustard seed, will continue to grow until it has branches in every nation, tribe and tongue. It advances through suffering servants who overcome by the death of their Master, who by the goodness of their lives disarm evil, hatred and violence and who by the word of their testimony and their willingness to die rather than to kill vanquish the falsehoods of the powerful. And one day his anger will be filled. The grapes of wrath will be poured out and those who have been faithful to the end will be saved and rule the earth.

This is the good news, the hope that we proclaim day-after-day to our friends involved in social work and community development, as we work together on issues of justice.

Political options

The following chart summarizes possible Christian responses to the injustices of squatter society. There are three main categories of response. The first category is that developed from seeing Christ as our model — a 'spiritual discipleship' model growing from Anabaptist, fundamentalist or Pentecostal roots.

The second category are responses that are developed from seeking to see the kingdom rule *over* or be expressed *in* every facet of human life. Here we recognize that Jesus chose to limit himself to an apostolic role — to a single human body, to a time, to a people, to a geography, to a three-year ministry. The role he chose was and is today the spearhead of establishing the kingdom.

Christian political options

1. 'Spiritual' discipleship model

INVOLVEMENT	HISTORICAL EXPRESSIONS	FOCUS OF ENERGY
Non-involvement in politics Involvement with the needy 'Spiritual' power struggles (the suffering Christ)	Under oppressive regimes (authorities controlled by demonic forces) Early church monastic orders Fundamentalists Mennonites Anabaptists	**In alternative structures:** Alternative communities demonstrating kingdom power in non-violence Ministry to the poor and needy Conflict with demonic forces in heavenly places

2. Holistic discipleship model

INVOLVEMENT	HISTORICAL EXPRESSIONS	FOCUS OF ENERGY
Alternative A: Political involvement, confrontation and reform of the power structures (Christ the Reformer) **Alternative B:** Involvement in the power structures with the ethically-based use of force or power (Christ the King)	Democracies Luther's attempts at an ordered society Franciscans The Salvation Army Tonga Calvin's Geneva	**In continuous reform of political structures:** Establishment of governments 'infiltrated' with kingdom ethics **In the control of political structures** Establishment of governments ruled by kingdom ethics

3. Christian deviations (non-Christian models using Christian language)

INVOLVEMENT	HISTORICAL EXPRESSIONS	FOCUS OF ENERGY
Alternative A: Abuse of power in the name of Christ (the 'Byzantine Christ' of purple and sceptre) **Alternative B:** Use of power against secular authorities Involvement in a power struggle with oppressive regimes (Christ the Zealot, Christ the humanitarian)	Christianized and post-Christian societies where the moral basis of the legitimate use of power has been destroyed, e.g. Cromwell Post-Constantine period Oppressive regimes 'Pax Marx' Liberation theology	**In acceptance of political structures:** Establishment of kingdom of God on earth by force and coercion. Perception of the kingdom of God as a servant of political structures. **In overthrow of political structures:** Establishment of kingdom of God on earth by force (where God's kingdom = revolutionary government) Identification of the 'principalities and powers' (Eph. 6:12) with corrupt political structures

RESPONSE TO VIOLENCE	SPECTRUM OF POLITICAL ACTION
Quietist approach Policy of non-resistance	Submit to authority. Pray for, those in authority. Live out the kingdom in alternative communities. Overcome evil with good, violence with pacifism and oppression with submission. Proclaim the gospel to the world. Separate oneself from the evil of the State (e.g. by refusal to worship the emperor, pay taxes for the military, serve in the army, act as a magistrate in a corrupt regime).

RESPONSE TO VIOLENCE	SPECTRUM OF POLITICAL ACTION
Activist approach Policy of non-violence Establishment approach Policy of violence or revolutionary violence	**Individual participation** in home, school, career and marketplace by: * exercising godly power (parental control, school discipline, communal authority) * ruling justly * promoting good legislation * being active in public office * organizing petitions and boycotts * promoting 'biblical' civil disobedience * protesting against evil by referring to one's constitutional rights. **Prophetic proclamation** (e.g. Solzhenitsyn) **Civil defence**

RESPONSE TO VIOLENCE	SPECTRUM OF POLITICAL ACTION
	Alternative A: Doctrine of just war. Civil religion. Suppression of all dissent in name of piety, stability and 'law and order'. Participation in exercise of amoral power, unjust rule and institutional evil. **Alternative B:** Protest of evil = unrequited bitterness Prophetic proclamation = 'conscientitization' Gospel of the kingdom = gospel of revolution Combat violence with violence Establish alternative revolutionary structures Rebel against corrupt authorities God is dead, therefore man is to destroy evil

INCREASING GROUP COMMITMENT TO AND COMPROMISE WITH NON-CHRISTIAN PHILOSOPHIES

But there are many other roles in the body of Christ. Principles can be seen in his life, but his practice, his methodology, his actions were an outworking only in that specific time, place and role. Category II considers Kingdom *principles* to be eternal, but *applications* to be time and culture-bound. All of the scriptures written across 2000 years need to be known and understood, if we would know what is right to do in any given time and place.

Because Jesus was not a lawyer does not imply no one should be lawyers (if you can grasp this triple negative). Because Jesus was not a community development worker does not imply there is no place for the Christian community development worker. Because he was not a politician does not imply Christians should give up politics.

Instead we must go to other scriptures which help us be a godly lawyer, community developer or politician. The principles lived out and taught by Jesus were also lived out by Moses the lawyer, Nehemiah the community developer, and Daniel the politician. God is unchangeable. His principles are unchangeable. Their application, however, varies from place to place, time to time.

One difference between category I and II in the chart is the understanding of power. Category I sees clearly that, since we are fighting against demonic forces and philosophies that have entered government, we need primarily to use spiritual warfare. For 'the weapons of our warfare are not physical, weapons of flesh and blood, but mighty before God for the overthrow and destruction of strongholds' (2 Corinthians 10:5, Amplified).

Prophets need such a biblical theology of power. Their power comes from the authority of a direct word from God. Part of such a biblical concept of power is the recognition that the power of God to heal the sick and set people free from demons is the spearhead of the kingdom of God.

Category II relates to those of us who are already in positions of political or economic power and need to learn the ethical uses of and limitations of such power. As citizens in semi-democratic societies, we need a biblical concept of how to fulfil our responsibilities. Some at times may be out demonstrating for an issue, others may be found praying, whilst others may believe that speaking directly the word of God to the politicians is more effective. Gandhi and Martin Luther King are our folk heroes in this. Numerous books discuss the issues involved.

Category III are non-biblical alternatives, resulting from using the scriptures to justify political viewpoints which themselves are not submitted to biblical authority.

Squatter Politics

What are the practical issues of justice for a worker in the slums?

1. Living amongst the poor is itself seen as a political action. It is interpreted by many as a symbol of siding with the poor against the oppression of the rich (the government consisting of the rich).

2. Establishing churches where people care for each other and treat each other justly is itself a deeply political action.

This involves proclamation, bringing reconciliation into families and between gangs, developing social activities and a social structure for the new believers and being involved in economic development projects and leadership training. The last two activities involve a healthy participation in the positive aspects of community development, relating with community leaders and with government agencies.

3. Public and private prayer for those in authority enables God to bring justice into society. It is a priority.

4. The Intelligence Service has a dossier on many Christian leaders in the Philippines, so one must always be very careful to check out activities with the Barrio leadership in order that any questions might be answered beforehand and all be above board. Interestingly, the people in Tatalon had come to hate the communist agitators — the community organizers that had come in and tried to stir up trouble back in the days when there was tremendous oppression in the community. They disliked their deceitfulness and bitterness.

At the same time, many had been unjustly treated by the government. One good friend was a leader of a women's auxiliary group in the community. She told me of the time some years before when she had organized the ladies group in the community and they had then gone and spoken to the Government officials to obtain basic services such as a water supply and road into the community.

But then that women's auxiliary had been drawn into a combination of anti-Marcos forces spearheaded by the priests and the Marxists. They had joined an illegal march and were arrested, incarcerated in Camp Crame for two days, and left to sleep on the floor. She did not understand why that had happened, but the emotional wound was very deep. She had not wanted to create trouble, but she had been led into trouble by these agitators. It's

184/With Justice for All

hard to be in the position of the poor in the Philippines!

5. Whilst avoiding aligning with any political faction in a community, it is good to build up community leaders. Respect, a winsome spirit and involvement with them at a practical level provide a basis for rapport, rebuke when they act corruptly, or consultation when the community is threatened.

6. Continued involvement in healing the sick, casting out demons and effecting changes by prayer pave the way also for exercising a prophetic ministry to community leaders. The dramatized prophetic word is a very biblical model.

7. The basic issue for squatters is to gain land rights for they dwell illegally. This involves speaking of an attitude of repentance towards oppressive landlords or government officials. Similar confrontations may develop over housing programs, water rights and sewerage.

8. Full participation in the life of the community by believers involves maintaining right relationships in home, school and office. It involves actively working at conciliation between groups within the community, or even protest to civil authorities through petitions and organised lobbying for land, employment, sewerage and so on. It will also involve a continued upgrading of the social responsibilities that people within the community feel towards each other in terms of policing crime, wiping out corruption and overseeing rubbish disposal and hygiene. This is a form of social or community organization. Opposition to the Marxists who will use this for their own ends is needed. Co-operation with the government upgrading program is to be encouraged as, in the main, these are well-intentioned in design and implementation.

9. The servant of God is not called to handle all these issues. He is called to handle those in which God wants him involved. Let me cite three areas of city-wide injustice, big enough for any one person to handle.

In July 1982, Madame Imelda Marcos began a new anti-squatting drive. The 'benevolent society' wished to clean up Manila, 'the City of Man'. Scores of thousands were loaded into trucks and deposited into relocation sites miles from the city — without water, without work, without promised facilities.[19]

Thus says the Lord; enough, O princes of Israel, put away violence and oppression, and execute justice and righteousness; cease your evictions of my people, says the Lord God (Ezekiel 45:9).

Who should speak this word and how can it be done in such a way to be received?

Or take the slave trade. It can only occur because the uppermost level of government officials protect it. Who dares take it on — at what level, and how?[20]

What about the exporting of Filipino labourers to the Middle East? It is one of the biggest forms of income for the squatters, but has led to thousands of situations of exploitation and trickery. Christian models of recruiting agencies need to be set up. Christian legislation needs introduction. Again, who will do it, and how?

Unattached!

Some will be frustrated with this chapter, for I have not outlined a comprehensive strategy to eliminate the slums. There is none. We are but a drop in the ocean of an insoluble problem. All that is written in the preceding pages comes out of ministry to people.

I picked up Malcolm Muggeridge's life of Mother Teresa and found that she too, while not neglecting programs, had concluded that the greatest gift was loving people, communicating to them their dignity and their worth, even when there was no final way to meet their physical needs. It is the transferral of the personal love and power of God that is ultimately of infinite and eternal value.

Involvement in people's lives results in different activities and responses in each community, for the needs differ. We will not solve the squatter problem, but we should do all in our power towards solving it. And we will dream of it.

Ultimately I dream of being given enough money to buy several hectares of land to do what Father Rafael Garcia-Harreros has done in Bogota: establishing a community of believers rescued from their poverty, enabling them to buy a piece of the land over time, build their own house and establish community structures and organization where 'justice will be the measuring line for the foundation and honesty will be its plumb line' (Isaiah 29:19). The goal is a restored community of redeemed people living under the rule of God.

But our dream we hold lightly for our eyes are fixed on an eternal city, whose designer and builder is God. While working with all the energy he inspires within us, we preach his kingdom to others and carve it into the structures of society here on earth. When the King returns, that kingdom of justice and righteousness will be fully established and it will be the end of those who oppress others and show contempt for God (Isaiah 29:19).

Unattached to this present world, as freely serve it, for love and justice compel. The vision of the holy city keeps us going in the midst of the privations and suffering. Even so, come quickly Lord Jesus.

Footnotes on Chapter 10

1. See also Waldron Scott, *Bring Forth Justice*, Eerdmans, 1980, pp 64-67
2. Jose Porfirio Miranda, *Marx and the Bible*, trans. John Eagleson, Maryknoll, Orbis Books, 1974, p 93
3. Celia T. Castillo, *Beyond Manila, Philippine Rural Problems in Perspective*, International Development Research Centre, Box 8500, Ottawa, Canada K1G 349, 1980)
4. *With Justice for All* by John Perkins, © Copyright 1982, Regal Books, Ventura CA 93006, p 105. Used by permission
5. Donald Durnbaugh, *Is 'Withdrawal' Involvement*, The Other Side, Box 158, Savannah, Ohio 44874, March-April 1974, pp 21-23
6. Alan R. Tippett, *People Movements in Southern Polynesia*, Moody Press, 1971
7. Ian Bradley, 'Saints against Sin', reprinted from the Observer in *The Other Side*, March-April, 1974, pp 24-27
8. McLelland, *Business Drive and National Achievement*, in 'Social Change', Etzioni and Etzioni pp 171 ff.
9. For a theological analysis of the problem of power see Martin Hengel, *Christ and Power*, trans. by Everett R. Kalin, Christian Journals (Ireland) Ltd, 1977
10. Xavier Leon Dujour S.J. *Saint Francis Xavier, The Mystical Progress of the Apostle*, Fr Henry Pascual Diz, S.J., St Paul Press Training School, Bandra, Bombay, 1950
11. For a broader discussion of Jesus' rejection of revolution see John H. Yoder, *The Original Revolution*, Herald Press, Scottdale, Pa. 15683, 1971, and Ronald Sider, *Christ and Violence*, Lion Publishing and Herald Press, 1979
12. Gustavo Gutierrez, *A Theology of Liberation*, Sr Caridad Inda and John Eagleson, trans. and eds. Maryknoll, Orbis Books, 1973
13. See Henrik Berkhof, *Christ and the Powers*, trans. John H. Yoder, Herald Press, 1962, 1977, for a theological analysis of the demonic in politics.
14. See Peter Beyerhaus, *Mission: Which Way, Humanization or Redemption*, Zondervan, 1971, for a fuller analysis. Also Bruce Nicholls, *Theological Reflections on Melbourne 1980* (mimeographed notes)

15. Piero Gheddo, *Why is the Third World Poor*, Orbis Books, 1973, for an insightful explanation of official Catholic and Biblical teaching, especially 'The Tragic Errors of Liberal Capitalism', pp 9-12
16. *With Justice for All* by John Perkins, © Copyright 1982 Regal Books, Ventura, CA 93006, p 102. Used by permission
17. Leon Morris, 'The Responsible Make Legends Happen', Christianity Today, September 7, 1979
18. Gheddo, *op. cit.*, pp 12-17
19. *Wretched of the Earth*, Concerned Citizens for the Urban Poor, Series 2, and Danilo-Luis M. Manano, *The Last Campaign*, Observer, Manila, 19 September 1982
20. Spencer Davidson and David De Voss, *Lust City in the Far East*, Time, May 10, 1982, or for fuller analyses Ron O'Grady *Third World Stopover*, WCC, 1981, and F. Landa Jocano, *Slums as a Way of Life*, chapter IX, University of the Philippines Press, 1975
21. Joy D. Palmer, Ross H. Munro, Adam Zagorin, 'They are Like Shadows', *Time*, 16 November, 1981

12
'Whom Will I Send?'
A VISION FOR REACHING ASIA'S URBAN POOR

HE WAS DRESSED IN THE JEANS, JANDALS AND T-SHIRT of the poor. Ten pastoral students lay around on the rocks, shaded from the dry, burning sun and listened, as he told us this story:

> There was a little city
> with a few men in it;
> and a great king came against it and besieged it,
> building great siegeworks against it.
> But there was found in it
> **a poor, wise man,**
> and he by his wisdom delivered the city.
> Yet no one remembered that poor man.
> But I say
> that wisdom is better than might,
> though the poor man's wisdom is despised,
> and his words are not heeded (Ecclesiastes 9:13-16).

This was the story of his life. This soft-spoken, bearded American had established a movement that had saved thousands, yet no one remembered him. This story from King Solomon became a centrepoint of a new movement to the slums from New Zealand churches.

Birth of a movement
It began one night in an evening of despairing prayer. Battered by reverse culture shock, by illness and the rejection of friends, I was wandering down a bush track in the evening sunlight. As I prayed,

God spoke through a picture in my mind: A brilliant picture, in a manner I've come to recognize as from God. He showed a hundred men and women wandering the byways of the slums, dwelling amongst the poor of ten great cities in Asia — poor wise men and women who would, as Wesley says, 'fear nothing but God and hate nothing but sin'. I saw a band of wandering apostles.

A woman artist living up the road dropped me a small note a few days later with a message the Lord had given her. It spoke of the same call. For some months I delayed: 'Lord, I have no contacts with the influential men of the church. Why call me to establish a movement? Physically I am sick! Emotionally, I am in shock! Socially, I have lost my friends!'

But the Lord continued to encourage. I determined not to visit the influential people, but to start where I was with what I had, and do what I could — for that is the way of a servant. I visited some friends. As I began to speak of the need, the Spirit of God was evident in unusual ways. People knew it was God's purpose. God led to many new groups.

Wherever I went, I found renewal. The renewal would break out wherever proud Christian leaders had humbled themselves before God. People would take me to meet such men. As I did, they would listen very humbly to this unknown missionary — and then they would confirm that this was God's voice and that he would raise up this work. God independently had spoken to many about the masses, the poor of Asia's cities. So a new missionary movement began.

Renewal in my home country has resulted in thousands of new converts — and the miracles, signs and gifts of a powerful God. There seem to be four phases of the renewal. The first is a phase of brokenness, humbling, repentance, restitution and seeking the Lord. As a result God has broken into people's lives in a new way with power, resulting in worship, evangelism and the exercise of spiritual gifts.

The second phase is a restructuring of traditional church life. House groups develop. Deep relationships and spiritual ministry to inner personal need occurs. Evangelism, flowing through normal social relationships, multiplies new believers. Where there is strong leadership training and disciplined intake of the word of God, the economic changes and care for the poor become part of a new pattern of life.

Four or five years after renewal of an older church or the birth of a new fellowship, a third phase emerges. Scores of people develop an eagerness to be involved in missions. Hundreds upon hundreds are volunteering for the field.

'Servants' was the name given to the new mission structure to accommodate the thrust to Asia's poor. It developed by God independently speaking to many of these churches. My role was to walk behind, sensing what God was doing and providing a structure to facilitate this thrust.

No unemployment

It was a poor man who saved the city. God looks for a hundred labourers. A hundred labourers means a hundred church-planters — people who can pioneer new fellowships in unreached areas.

Leaders don't grow on trees. It takes eight or nine years of mature training in a dynamic church situation to produce such a man.

Along with these church-planters, we need women with a depth of godly character, developed leadership and ministry skills and the ability to function as part of church-planting teams.

Such a task requires all the social, intellectual and spiritual capacities a person has. No lifestyle can match the thrill of church-planting. None demand so much from a person.

But renewal, the power of God and his miraculous signs, will not alone produce such men and women. If we would develop long-term cross-cultural missionaries, the critical element is *apprenticeship relationships*. Elisha, apprentice to Elijah, received a double portion of Elijah's spirit. Joshua, forty years' servant of Moses, led the people into Israel. Paul could say of Timothy: 'I have no-one else like him, who is genuinely interested in your welfare.'

Restructured churches need not only new pastoral evangelistic house-group structures. They need encouragement to develop this apprenticeship model of training labourers. In the past this has been a unique contribution of a number of para-church organizations in the body of Christ. Unfortunately over a period of time they have become culturally cut off from the mainstream of the Holy Spirit's renewal in New Zealand church life. Time may cause a wider identification with the main thrusts of God's work throughout the country.

In the meantime a number of old friends encouraged me. They had grasped the church growth and training principles inherent in the Navigator model in which we grew up. As men and women were called by God to the work amongst the poor, I would sit down with their pastor and elders and discuss with them principles and phases of training potential labourers. Pastors were excited to see a new pattern of ministry opening up before them. Theologically the pastors had moved to a commitment to training. They appreciated practical input that helped them implement the new theology. I adapted the 'Focus Chart' developed by Gene Tabor. It came to be known as 'The Four Seasons of Christian Training'.

Rather than giving a program of training as most groups do, it gives principles or foci at each of the four commonly identifiable stages of growth of a potential worker. The pastors and elders in every situation spent considerable time in enthusiastic discussion as to what stages they were in and what were next steps of growth.

The first phase is a healthy Christian 'babyhood' in a warm, relational, celebrating home-group and church fellowship. Most growing churches had become skilled in this.

The second phase requires more personal discipling of the person by an elder or house group leader in the context of ministering to a small group of other believers.

The third phase is the involvement of disciples in ministry to others as part of the church's ministry team — as house-group leaders, as youth leaders, as part of the counselling or outreach team and so on. Even the leader of a creche can easily turn this role of involving and personally discipling young mothers.

During this phase of ministry the critical element is development of character. Potential leaders need to meet at least fortnightly for ministering to each other at the personal level, relating scriptural teaching to the problems or matters that have merged in the past fortnight.

The fourth phase of training focuses on development of gifts and calling. For men it normally involves a semi-independent ministry: establishing a church, or pioneering a new ministry thrust. For women it requires experience working in a leadership team developing this kind of ministry thrust.

Robin and his merry men

But there is another kind of labourer in the scriptures — men and women skilled as deacons and deaconesses. For we not only need the apostle, the pastor-teacher or evangelist; we need men and women filled with the Holy Spirit and with wisdom, who are skilled in using money given by the rich to meet the needs of the poor. (The early deacons did not give out hymnals at the door!)

We need men skilled in establishing small scale industries: carpentry shops, electronics shops and machine shops. We need men and women skilled in social work, administration and community development. It would seem that couples in their forties and fifties whose children are now independent are the best possible people for such tasks.

Wisdom

The poor man who saved the city was wise. Such wisdom is not primarily learned in school. Christ imparted his wisdom in the context of loving action. For wisdom has to do with character, decision-making, ethical issues, relationships. Theology, the knowledge of God, is moral. Learning about the God of history as he works today is possible only through involvement in history.

Yet godly wisdom is not only 'heard along the streets'. As Solomon adds, wisdom is based on 'getting knowledge, getting understanding'. That means it has an intellectual component.

The mission field needs trained tradesmen. It also needs men and women of the finest academic training. To know when and how to rebuke in another culture requires cultural understanding. To understand the culture sufficiently to mobilize a movement requires the finest training in mastering language, culture missions theory and church history.

How to appoint eldership is a profound theological question in the slums where few men are living with their first wife. Community development and church growth principles require mastering if the kingdom would be established over a community. The complexity of issues is unending.

We must upgrade Australasia's training schools to provide the best postgraduate evangelical training in such areas. We must renounce the anti-intellectualism inherent in fundamentalism (despite its penchant for academic degrees and titles!) and in our culture. It is unbiblical.

Most workers need to be able to grapple with the concepts of the scriptures. But their teaching will not be by books and concepts, but, as with the Master, by story and parable. The ability to tell stories grows out of a full-orbed life. The skilled non-academic tradesman usually is better at this than the scholar. We need tradesmen and scholars who are socially balanced, personally mature and professionally equipped.

At the same time God's wisdom is not primarily academic. It comes from the Spirit revealing the mind of Christ. Finely trained minds are the outworking of spiritual discernment. Workers need to have discernment concerning the leading of the spirit. They need to know how to exercise spiritual gifts in confrontation with the demonic, in healing the sick, in prophecy or through a (supernatural) word of discernment, word of knowledge or interpretation of dreams.

Above all they need to be men and women of the word of God. It is possible as a layman over five or six years to do an in-depth study of all of the scriptures and to memorize several hundred passages that will transform one's thinking patterns.

The missionary needs to be a person of balance — sound in theology, bold and authoritative, but meek and flexible; able to exercise spiritual gifts and power, but not extremist; fully developing his academic capacities, but deeply spiritual and pragmatic.

More important than academic ability is having a fine sensitivity, an ability to feel what others around are feeling, able to be a leader from the midst of the people, able to incarnate a people's soul, to speak their poetry and their aspirations.

This is the gift of cross-cultural communication! It requires a strength of will on the inside, an inner fibre coupled with above-average sensitivity, flexibility and adaptability. It involves a capacity for suspended judgement — being able to hold two opposing views in one's mind without getting under tension. The black-and-white absolutist or judgemental thinker is not a natural missionary. One who has an ear for music will have a reasonable ear for language. A cross-cultural worker will also at some stage have studied linguistics and anthropology.

Above all, the cross-cultural worker is one who has learned Jesus — who loves him, knows him and understands his reactions. those who display the character of Christ given in the Sermon on the Mount are well able to cross cultures. Perhaps to memorize that sermon is the place to begin.

Missionary school

The schooling of such a man or woman is in sending them to find alcoholics, to rescue lesbians and homosexuals, to walk for months with the drug addict, to spend long nights explaining the gospel to abusive students, to live amongst the poorest immigrant community and heal prejudice, to evangelize the prisons and the bikies. The harder the sufferings encountered in our pleasant Western society, the more equipped will that person be.

Only those with the power of submission, those able to trust others with decisions about their lives, will survive the tensions of a mission community. Such lessons must be learned *before* reaching the field. Potential missionaries should be taught to live without possessions (except books, since these contribute to wisdom, and tools of the trade). They should master a trade or career. They should learn to eat little meat and few desserts, to know how to keep their body healthy through wise diet, natural foods, the use of herbs and good exercise. They should practise living in crowded conditions and coping with constant pressures.

They should study the lives of those who have preceded them amongst the poor: Hudson Taylor, Xavier, Assissi or Mother Teresa, Amy Carmichael, Sadhu Sundar Singh and so on. They should grapple with the social implications of the gospel in their own country in order to have a basis for grappling with it elsewhere, where possible picking up social work and community development skills. For the missionary in the slums will find life far less comfortable than in some remote village. In a village he does not share his life with social equals and so in his visits to the city he can reassume his Western roles. But the slum missionary must simultaneously maintain satisfactory relationships both with the slum-dwellers and with mentors and officials in the local university and government. He wears several hats.

Francis Xavier was insistent on tested men. He suggested the following tests for potential missionaries:

> The spiritual exercises will be made for a month, in order to judge the nature of the individual, his steadfastness, temperament, inclinations and vocation. For another month he will serve the poor in the hospitals in every kind of menial work he might be ordered to perform, because to humble oneself in all meekness and care nothing for the esteem of the world is to set at naught human respect. During the third month, he must make a pilgrimage on foot and without money, placing his entire hope in the Creator and Lord, accustoming himself to bad food and a comfortless bed. He who cannot either rest or travel without food and with poor sleep for twenty-four hours will be unable, we believe, to persevere in the Society.[1]

It was not enough to Xavier for men to have spiritual yearnings and deceptive dreams; they needed to pass these tests as well. The harvest is urgent, but God takes his time to train his harvesters.

Sacrifice

The call is also costly in terms of family relationships, separation from children and health. 'How lonesome the weary hours confined to my room,' wrote Hudson Taylor upon the death of his wife. 'How I missed my dear wife and the little pattering footsteps of the children far away in England.' While God never calls us to desert our family responsibilities, he may, for a limited season, call us to sever those links. Certainly sickness or death by natural causes hastens on the experience of dislocation.

Most great mission leaders, whilst knowing God's power in prayer for the sick, were often sickly themselves: living in difficult climates, in situations of poorly controlled hygiene.

All extension of the kingdom is accomplished at cost. Yet the Lord is no man's debtor. Our children, our wives and our husbands are his. He holds them in his hands.

Kagawa wrote this poem to his wife:

> You who dwell
> In the heart of my heart
> Listen to me;
> This you must know —
> I am a child of grief and pain
> Bending my fingers to count my woe.
> You yield me
> everything;
> But I
> have nothing
> I can bring
> To give to you.
> Know
> You have married
> Poverty, sorrow;
> Bear it with me;
> The storm will be over
> Tomorrow.
> A little while
> For us
> The rod;
> And then,
> Then God.[2]

And Haru his wife had married not only poverty and sorrow. She had married a man who would always be wandering.

For many, work in the slums is a call to celibacy. For others, to a lifestyle of singleness for some years. This call to singleness is not a call to individualism, but to a mobile and sacrificial community, to a sharing of one's life with a team because of mutual commitment to a task that demands freedom from family responsibilities. Singleness in the ancient orders involved vows of chastity. This commitment to chastity, or as we call it purity of heart, is contrary to all the tendencies of nature. Chosen singleness is not a breaking of human affections. It is chosen that we might be available to love our neighbour more fully. To be unloving leaves us heavily burdened. It is a calling in God's economy, enabling people to more deeply know their Lord. Many people give their early years to the pursuit of love; we must give it to the pursuit of God.

A poor man

The wise man who saved cities was also poor. The missionary of today is one who can support himself and others from a trade or profession. His choice of poverty is not a choice of dependency.

His poverty is chosen as a sign of love, as a sign of justice. It is not to be a burden, but to bring joy! It is to set free for it is freely chosen! It is a choice of liberty and joy, for the spirit of simplicity does not consist of pursuing misery.

Such 'labouring poverty' cannot be legislated by the rules of a mission. It is chosen freely by those who know that, having forsaken wealth, they cannot be bought by money; having forsaken power, position and influence, they cannot be bought by influence; having forsaken all security, they cannot be bought by the offer of security.

In such a lifestyle and commitment it is hard to persevere. The enthusiasm of the early days passes away; easier courses appear; the capacity to suffer often decreases as one suffers. Idealism is easily blunted on reality and its bluntening may either bring balance or turn one back from the earlier ideal. And the constant glitter of the cities in which we dwell subtly brings captivity to the desire for things.

The Apostle Peter struggled, too. He once questioned Jesus, 'Look, Lord, we've left everything to follow you. What is our portion? What do we get out of it?'

Jesus did not rebuke the sanity of his question, but replied,

'There is no one who has left house or brothers and sisters or
mother or father or children or lands for my sake and for the
gospel, who will not receive a hundredfold now in this time,
houses and brothers and sisters and mothers and children and
lands, with persecutions and, in the age to come, eternal life'
(Mark 10:28-30).

The movement
Behind such a mission thrust of poor, wise men and women there
needs to grow a movement of hundreds of men and women in the
sending base who are choosing another sort of poverty — that of
simplicity.

This is the commitment of my home church. It has over thirty
missionaries. The means of supporting them? Simplicity!

One church leader has chosen to limit his engineering business
activities to those necessary to supplying his basic needs — in
order to be free to devote himself to the business of the kingdom.
Yet others have given themselves to making money to give to
missions. Some have chosen homes half as expensive as they
formerly owned. Some have sat down and calculated each area of
their expenses, each item in their possession, sold the excess items
and given to the poor. Many women have given their best clothes
to the poor. Some have sold their jewellery. One couple in
response to the Lord's prompting gave a welding machine for the
poor in the slums.

These are ordinary men and women 'living simply that others
may simply live', living frugally that missionaries may be provided
sufficiently to continue spearheading the kingdom, living without
in order that they be victorious in the fight against the demon of
affluence — the demon of the 'half gallon, quarter-acre, pavlova
paradise' which controls our nation.

Many are choosing to live out their simplicity communally with
other believers in order to break down the twin brother of this
devilish affluence, excessive individualism. It has destroyed not
only our society, but our nuclear family structures. It is the cause
of the new poverty of urban New Zealand. The same pattern holds
for other Western countries as well. How do they live
communally? The most effective communal structure has been the
house group, a weekly meeting of six to fifteen people learning to
mould their lives to be 'family' one to the other, seeking to hear
God's direction, worshipping and studying the word together. It
enables its members to live within existing Western culture whilst

beginning to learn the social and economic implications of the kingdom. Sharing of economic problems, recreation together, sharing of garden tools, meals, vehicles and ministry all grow naturally from this.

Many believers move from this to adding semi-detached quarters to their home: for a solo mum, a widow or single young folk. Others have obtained three or four houses close to each other in the same street in order to share the load of hospitality, child supervision and possessions. Landed communities have developed, but few have been successful. It is widely debated if such a concept is encouraged in the scriptures.

It is such groups of believers who will lead the church in any coming time of economic collapse. Rejecting affluence and individualism now is a costly discipline. But they will be ready and equipped to minister to shattered unbelievers during a time of collapse and will reap a great harvest for their steadfastness.

It is from such groups that missionaries are being equipped. Would that all of our churches repent of their dependence on wealth and of allowing the business ethic to lead and control them. God will judge these sins!

Along with such communities of committed believers, God longs to raise up a band of praying women who will give their lives to prayer for the slums. An old lady of eighty-four has prayed daily for me these thirteen years. Another of twenty-eight has chosen to work half time and give her life to prayer... A band of ladies in my church are known as women of intercession.

This is the pattern of history. The nunneries we often joke about have been the source of power for numerous movements. Assissi and his men in times of confusion and uncertainty would repair to Saint Clara and her sisters to have these cloistered women seek the Lord's will on their behalf!

Momentum

The poor of Asia's cities — this is the great thrust of mission in the next twenty years.

The first team has been sent. Thirty others are in training. In each city prayer groups have emerged, committed not only to weekly or fortnightly evenings of prayer, usually fasting over tea, but to involvement in thinking through the issues of justice in our society in its relationship to the Third World and in small ways to ministering to the poor. They also provide a central support group for those who are in training under their church elders.

Other missions have also heard the cry of the poor of the cities. Others are speaking the same message. God has initiated the thrust; God is developing it. We need to walk with God into it.

Coming full circle

Milleth had just taught us a Jewish dance. Everybody was rejoicing. The late afternoon shadows rustled back and forth in the wind. Sito announced our special guest — Aling Nena!

She stood up in her finest dress. She had just had her teeth removed. She smiled in embarrassment. Then in clear Tagalog she told her story.

'I used to be a gambler and a drunkard... (Everybody around knew the past.)

'Now my life is changed. (Everybody around knew the change.) It's Jesus who has done it...

'What I want to do now is to go to those poor people who live on the rubbish dump and preach to them about Jesus. They are poorer than we are. I want them to know what Jesus can do...'

And so the kingdom spreads.

* * *

Seventy people from around New Zealand gathered in prayer, worshipping God. Seven had just been commissioned to Asia's slums. The next morning others would assemble early to commit themselves for training to go. As we sang, a picture of the Lord came to mind.

He came from Mount Zion on a magnificent white charger. As from a distance he descended upon one of the great cities of Asia, the millions of its inhabitants lined its streets, all worshipping God in song and dance.

Every man amongst them had a home. There seemed to be no rich, no poor. All left their work to worship the King.

And in the city gates, in the midst of the crowd, was a wizened, simply-garbed man leaning on his staff — not noticeably different from the crowd. But as the King swept through the gates, he paused and, looking across the crowd, greeted the servant with a smile, a nod and a 'well done'. Then the King continued on his way as the millions delighted with him. And the servant of the city was content with his labour.

* * *

Footnotes on Chapter 12

1. Xavier Leon Du Jour, S.J., *St Francis Xavier*, pp 65, 66 — trans. Henry Pascual Oiz, S.J., St Paul Press Training School, Bandra, Bombay, 1950
2. Toyohiko Kagawa, 'The Cross of the Whole Christ', in *Meditations on the Cross*, SCM, 1936

For further information on the work of the new mission SERVANTS TO ASIA'S URBAN POOR or for further information on training for urban missionary work in Asia, please write to:

> N.Z. Co-ordinator
> Servants
> PO Box 3038
> Christchurch
> New Zealand